MW00334750

VET Tv's Military Slang Dictionary

by
Veteran Television

Thanks to all the men and women who accidentally gave birth to children they weren't ready to raise. You have kept the U.S. military stocked with wanna-be alphas who spend their lives trying to forget about their shitty childhoods and need VET Tv to stay sane.

No, seriously, thank you.

THANK YOU TO ALL CONTRIBUTORS

John Acevedo   Freddy Lopez
Ben Alvarado   Jessica Mandala
Jacob Aronen   Emily McGuiness
Jeff Brandimarte   Kevin McNease
Logan Coble   Chris Michael
Cody Dobbins   Brandon Monger
Emily Everett   Lynn Nix
Josh Flanagan   Donny O'Malley
Ashley Ford   Matthew Owen
Jon Forsythe   Justice Pelton
Josh Francis   Fernando Rivera
James Green   Sarah Sahutske
Matt Jimenez   Matt Shaddox
Greg Kelly   Dan Shankle
Matiyes Kinker   Levi Smock
Zachery Laning   Seth Stockmaster
Ethan Long   Scott Yoffe

Edited by Reese Johnson
Illustrations by Daniel Donnelly
Designed by Finn Paige

Follow, Tag & Share

VETERAN TELEVISION

At VET Tv, we create entertainment that recreates and parodies the military experience in order to build a community and prevent veteran suicide. We joke about all the things that civilians think are sacred. Why? Because in the military, nothing is sacred.

VeteranTv.com
Subscribe or Die

Download the free VET Tv app today and start streaming on all your favorite devices.

Official VET Tv Drinking Game

1. All players gather in a circle.

2. The personal holding the *Military Slang Dictionary* (MSD) is the Master of Ceremonies.

3. The person across from them is the Private.

4. Master of Ceremonies' job is to find a random word in the MSD and say that word out loud.

5. Private has to try to guess the definition of the random word.

6. If the Private gets it right, they take a drink. Private has two options with each drink they accumulate: Private can stop and give that one drink away or Private can keep guessing definitions.

7. For every correct answer, Private accumulates one more drink to give away. But if Private is wrong, they have to drink all of the accumulated drinks themselves. High risk, high reward.

8. Five drinks is an automatic shotgun.

9. After each round, the roles move counterclockwise.

10. Keep going in circles until it's time to go out or until you can't walk anymore!

General Orders

1. Take charge of this post and all gov't property
    in view that I personally see value in. Nothing more,
    nothing less.

2. Walk my post like a boss, stay on top o' shit, and
    observe a few of the things that take place within
    sight or hearing with my headphones on.

3. Report the violations of orders that I agree with
    and don't think are stupid.

4. Repeat all calls more distant from the guardhouse
    than my own.

5. Quit my post only when my replacement is getting
    dressed and is a few moments away from taking over.

6. To receive, consider, and (if I find it to be valuable),
    pass on to the sentry who relieves me some orders from
    the commanding officer, officer of the day, officers, and
    non-commissioned officers of the guard only.

7. Talk to no one but my homies while in the line
    of duty. It's all fun and games when on duty, until
    someone catches you and chews you out.

8. Scream for help if I think there's a slight commotion.
    My senior enlisted will applaud me for being vigilant
    and taking decisive action.

9. Text one of my homies if I don't know what to do.

10. Salute some of the officers I respect and all colors that
    have no wrinkles or blemishes.

11. Be especially watchful at night, when the OOD could
    sneak up on you at any moment. If homies step up, put
    em' in their place. If they get really loud, blast em'.
    Ain't nobody got time fo' dat.

72

Three-day weekend or 72 hours of liberty. Not enough time for drugs to exit your system. Be prepared for a piss test on return.

96

Four-day weekend or 96 hours of liberty. Almost enough time for drugs to exit your system. Be prepared for a piss test on return.

99

A message for all hands.

4/10/04

A female who is usually a 4 but becomes a 10 on deployment.

(INSERT REMAINING DAYS) & A WAKE UP

Number of days until you are free. Could include deployment, basic training port calls. Really any time you feel like you are trapped and in prison and are days away from killing yourself.

...OR SOME SHIT

The tail end of sentence when you don't really know what you're talking about but trying to sound like you do...or some shit.

1 FOR CHESTY

When a Marine is doing any sort of physical exertion that involves reps. This includes pull-ups and crunches that max out the PFT. The Marine, after maxing his score, does an extra rep in honor of the badass "Chesty Puller."

1-PUMP CHUMP

An individual who can't stroke his penis more than one time before blowing his load. Also the guy who only did one deployment.

1...1...1...1...1...

What the asshole who is supposed to be counting your repetitions during PT says when he/she doesn't think your last rep counted and wants to see you suffer, because everyone is secretly a sadist.

10-POUND HEAD

Stubborn. Ten pounds of smashed asshole in a five-pound sack. See 8 Up or Ate Up.

10 UP, 2 DOWN

See 8 Up or Ate Up.

100 FEET OF FLIGHT LINE

Imaginary flight line.
Typically used to trick the
new guy into thinking it's
a real thing.

100 MILE AN HOUR TAPE

Adhesive tape used by the
military, ordered from
an unknown location, that
posesses the ability to hold
together aircraft for years
on end yet cannot hold up a
poster on drywall.

10-4 FUCK OVER

What you say back to the
SOG when he's giving stupid
commands over the radio

11B PROOF

Something so durable/easy
even an 11B couldn't possibly
fuck it up.

12 ON 12 OFF

Work schedule equating to 12
hours on and 12 hours off.
Just hope you don't have to
hot rack.

12TH GENERAL ORDER

The made up 12th General
Order for a sentry: To walk
my post from flank to flank and
take no shit from any rank.

15 MIN EARLY TO 15 MIN EARLY

If you're 15 minutes early,
you're right on time, so you
must be 15 minutes earlier
than that to actually be 15
minutes early. Most humans
Call this "30 minutes early."

15 MINUTES PRIOR

Fifteen minutes early. If
you're 14 minutes 59 seconds
(or less) early, you're late.

15 MINUTES PRIOR TO 15 MINUTES PRIOR TO INFINITY

When no one knows the actual
time of the event so everyone
deducts 15 minutes each
time word is passed down
just to cover their asses,
causing everyone to be
different levels of earliness
and, ironically, wasting
everyone's time even more.

15-6

Formal investigation.
Basis for UCMJ, so basically
you're fucked.

1ST CIV DIV

The imaginary unit you join
when you become a civilian.

1ST LT

The second lieutenant who
actually survived a land
nav course to make it to
his next promotion.

1ST SARNT

Army first sergeants.

1ST SAUSAGE

Derogatory term for
an Army first sergeant.

1ST SGT'S FUCK DOLL

A junior enlisted military
member preyed on by the
company first sergeant.

2 SCOOPS OF HOOAH

An imaginary supplement a
soldier takes for motivation.

29 STUMPS

Twentynine Palms, California:
the Marine Corps' worst duty
station in the middle of the
desert. Sometimes referred to
as "Satan's Butthole."

2ND LT

See Butter Bar.

3 TO A PISSER

Men who go to Boot camp
quickly learn that time is
a luxury they are no longer
afforded. When you get a
moment to go to the head,
you fit as many swinging dicks
per pisser as you can.
Not limited to three.

30K MILLIONAIRE

The bonus a service member
receives for signing up for
another four years, balls
out, and is broke six months
later.

32% APR

The standard rate any dumb
boot gets from the used car
lot just off base and thinks
it's a sweet deal because
this is their first car and
they finally have money to
spend.

3RD DECK FLIGHT CREW

Someone who is suicidal on
the ship or in the barracks
and may jump off from the
third deck into the water
or onto the concrete.

4-WALL COUNSELING

Beating the shit out of
someone to prove a point or
as part of a lesson. Not to
be confused with hazing.

40 MIKE-MIKE

A 40-millimeter grenade that gets shot out of Mk-19 and M-203 grenade launchers to fuck up your target and everything around it.

45 AND 45

A 45-day restriction with 45-day pay reduction as punishment for violating the UCMJ. Usually accompanied by loss of rank.

4TH POINT OF CONTACT

"How about you get your head out of your ass?"

5-FINGER DISCOUNT

See Tactically Acquired.

5 FINGERS OF DEATH

A fist.

5-JUMP CHUMP

Silver Airborne wings: you've only done five jumps.

50 FT. OF CHOW LINE

Fake object to fuck with new guys.

550 CORD

Paracord commonly used by paratroopers. One of the most versatile ropes used for anything from securing loose gear or tying the new guys together so they don't get lost.

5S AND 25S

Tactical maneuver when exiting a vehicle where you check for "surprise presents" left by terrorists that you might step on in five- and 25-meter radii.

7 DAY

A store where you buy condoms you're probably not going to use anyways.

7 TONS OF FUN

Literally anything but fun, in fact, the worst possible thing.

75TH SICK CALL RANGER REGIMENT

A unit full of broke-dick injured people and fat-bodies.

782 GEAR

See Deuce Gear.

8 UP

That one dirtbag who is just a waste of human life.

8-YEAR SPECIALIST

A specialist who reenlisted but is a total fuck up. They will never see any NCO rank.

90/10

90% woman, 10% male. Chick with a dick. Usually from Thailand.

99Z

The MOS designated to shammers, dirtbags and terminal E-4s.

A TO B

To quickly summarize how to navigate from location to location.

ABORTION

An operation that was a complete disaster and nothing went as planned.

ABOVE MY PAY GRADE

Shit that you don't want to deal with so you leave it up to someone with a higher ranking to deal with.

ACQUIRE

The active means of obtaining equipment or tools that do not belong to you.

ACT A FOOL

When you know what's going on or are capable of handling something but act as if you are clueless to get out of it.

ACTUAL FUCK

A phrase to stress just how fucked a situation is.

AFGHAN GOGGLES

Nostalgia you feel towards the best and worst times of your life during a deployment to Afghanistan.

AFI

"Another Fucking Inconvenience." A term used when something screws up your day.

AFT

Backside of a ship. The direction facing your six.

A-GANG

The auxiliary division onboard a ship or sub responsible for sanity, HVAC, emergency diesel, hyds and other important systems.

AIDS MARINES

Landing support specialist Marines. While they occasionally help load and unload helicopters, you will usually find them at their weekly beach BBQ on Camp Pendleton or sleeping in a storage container while someone else is doing their job. They can be distinguished by the red tabs on their cammies which are intended to identify them as people in charge of assisting with beach landings, but in reality, serve as an identifier that their personality is total AIDS.

AIR ASSAULT

One of the easiest schools in the military. Anyone can get this badge.

AIR BEAR

Air Force security forces.

AIR FORCE

The branch of service in the military that everyone is jealous of.

AIR FORCE GLOVES

Pockets. Also known as Air Force mittens.

AIR GRUNTS

A-10 pilots, AKA "Grunts of the Air."

AIR PICKET

Airborne system tasked with detecting, reporting and tracking enemy air assets.

AIR SHARK

WW2 planes from the P40 through the P51.

AIRBORNE

Soldiers who jump from perfectly good airplanes for $150 a month.

AIRBORNE KNEE

Jacked up knees from "great" parachute landings.

AIRDALE

Aviation rates and aircrew.

ALABASTER CHROME

Commander General 2nd Class of Checkpoint Charlie (1&2).

ALI BABA

Local Iraqi thieves, insurgents, or looters.

ALIBI

Marrying a woman because you don't want people to know you're gay.

ALL PRESENT OR ACCOUNTED FOR

A phrase used to indicate that everyone is present at an event or formation. Whether it's true or not doesn't matter.

ALOHA SNACKBAR

Making fun of jihadist's "Allahu Akbar" chant.

ALPHA CHARLIE

"Ass-chewing."

ALPHA MIKE FOXTROT

"Adios, Motherfucker."

ALPHA ROSTER

Alphabetical list of everyone in the unit and their contact information.

ANAL CREAMPIE

Loads of semen oozing out of one's butthole.

ANAL SANDWICH

Anal double-penetration.

ANCHOR CLANKER

Any chief petty officer whose insignia is an anchor.

ANGRY BOTTOM

A gay man who is ashamed of liking it in the butt.

ANTEATER

Uncircumcized penis skin.

ANYMOUSE

Sailors' "anonymous" suggestions box.

ARCTIC SLIPPER

A cold weather "Pocket Pussy."

AREA BEAUTIFICATION

The cyclic tasking of improving one's surroundings to include, but not limited to pulling weeds and sweeping dirt. Based on guidance of an unknown source who decided it was better than training.

ARMOR TEST

When you are wearing your plate carrier with SAPI plates and someone Spartan kicks you to "test" the proper functionality of the armor.

ARMY

The largest branch of the American armed forces which all the dudes who "almost joined the Marines" enlisted.

ARMY PROOF

Fool proof.
Impossible to fuck up.

ARTICLE 134

A catch-all article in the UCMJ for offenses that are not spelled out elsewhere but they really want to fuck you over for something.

ARTICLE 15

An "unbiased" way for a servicemember to be judged by their commanding officer for an offense that doesn't require judicial intervention.

AS I WAS

A term only fucking idiots use to correct themselves. To return to what you were doing. Another way of saying, "disregard my last."

AS YOU WERE

A dumbass way to tell other service members to disregard the last command and continue what they were doing.

ASS BREATH

Foul-smelling breath. Usually after giving a rim job.

ASS CHEWING

A severe verbal reprimand from a superior. Usually for a stupid reason or for sheer lack of competence from the individual receiving it.

ASS CHUNKS

Pieces of butt meat that resemble ground beef.

ASS CLOWN

Another name to call people who are fucking retards, just in a nicer form.

ASS DOUCHE

A generally pleasant-smelling liquid designed to freshen up the colon.

ASS GASKET

Disposable paper ring on a public toilet.

ASS HAT

Another name to call people who are fucking retards, in a nicer form.

ASSED UP

Not up to standard, be it uniform appearance, attitude, following orders, etc.

ASSES AND ELBOWS

When everyone is super busy.

ASSFUCKERY

The ultimate fuck up, typically by SNCOs from the South.

ASSHOLE TO BELLY BUTTON

Commonly used when round-stepping or humping in formation to encourage the troops to stay as close as possible to the person in front of them. Also known as Nut to Butt in the male platoon.

ASS MAN

Someone's sexual preference between asses and boobs.

ASTRONAUT

Trainee who is so bad he orbits the whole squadron until he ends up with his original technical instructors.

ASVAB WAIVER

An incredibly dumb service member.

ASVAB WARRIOR

An incredibly dumb servicemember who is only qualified for the infantry.

ATE UP

That dirtbag soldier who doesn't get right no matter what you do to fix them.

ATOMIC SIT-UP

A prank where someone is challenged to do a sit-up blindfolded. While laying on the ground blindfolded, another person stands above them with their bare ass exposed. When the situp is attempted, the blindfold is removed, sending the person's face into the other person's ass.

ATTENTION TO DETAIL

The closeness of attention to which a servicemember pays the subject.

AYE HERO

A sarcastic, negative way
to address someone who is
doing something potentially
dangerous.

AYE MARINE

A greeting to let a Marine
know they are fucked up.

B HOLE JUSTICE

Revenge fuck after your
girlfriend cheats on you
with Jody.

B1RD

Mispelling of bird.

BA 1100N

A way to get rid of a
new guy by making them do
busy work. "Bee Ay Eleven
Hundred November."

BA-11S

A man's balls.

BABY ARM

When you've got a cock so
big it literally looks like
the arm of a baby attached
to your pelvis.

BABY BEATER

Small hammer used for repairs
on a Navy vessel.

BABY DICKS

The compilation of military
members with the smallest
cocks in the platoon, all of
whom somehow have incredibly
attractive girlfriends.

BABY SHIT

Paint remover.

BABY WIPES

Sanitary wipes. Substitutes for a shower in the field. Also used to clean your rifle.

BACK 40

The backside of base, or the wooded side of the base.

BACK AT BRAGG

When you were at Ft. Bragg.

BACK OFFICE

Ass.

BACON

Breakfast pork strips.

BAD JUJU

Superstitious term used to describe a string of bad luck.

BAD LARRY

Something cool.

BAG DADDY

Tactical.

BAG DRAG

Dipping your balls in the open mouth of a sleeping individual.

BAG NASTY

A terrible sack lunch. Usually composed of a two-day-old warm ham sandwich, fruit and a watered-down juice drink.

BAG OF ASS

When you look like shit, most notably your uniform. It may be because you were drinking with machine gunners the night before, or it may be you're just a shitbag who doesn't give a fuck if your uniform looks like total ass.

BAG OF BROKEN DICKS

A gathering of military members on light duty.

BAG OF DICKS

See Bag of Ass.

BAG OF SMASHED HOLES

A gathering of strippers in the barracks.

BALLS

Midnight. Called balls
because 0000 looks like
two sets of balls.

BALLS TO 8

The midnight-to-0800 watch.

BAM

Broad-assed Marine (female).
A female Marine with a
dumptruck of an ass.
You would eat her shitter
like an apple fritter.

BAMCIS

The six troop-leading steps.
However, this is usually
a phrase exclaimed by a
Marine who accomplished
a complicated task.

BAMF

"Bad-Ass Motherfucker."

BANANA SHOW

For those lucky enough to be
sent to Southeast Asia, you
will observe small Asian women
performing sex acts with their
vaginas that must be seen to
be believed. One of these acts
entails a woman inserting a
whole banana into her pussy
and pushing it out sliced.

BANDINI

The lake at Twentynine Palms
which emits the most foul
stench that adds to the
misery of being stationed
at Twentynine Palms.

BANG BANG SWITCH

To sexually pass a group of
strippers between military
members.

BANG SWITCH

The trigger of your weapon.

BARNEY STYLE

When you are trying to
explain something but your
audience (probably Marines)
is too dumb to understand
what you are saying, so you
have to break it down into
terms that even a small child
would understand.

BARRACKS BARBER

The dude who cuts hair in
the barracks. Frowned upon
by command, but sometimes
necessary if it's Sunday
night when the barber shops
are closed and you don't want
an ass-chewing at Monday
formation. The chances of
you getting a good haircut
increase exponentially if
he's Mexican.

BARRACKS BASH

Can happen anytime Marines
obtain liberty. Always
involves alcohol, underage
consumption, fights,
gangbangs, duty logs and
alleged sexual misconduct
with possible false rape
accusations. Occurs usually
two to three times per week,
but can fluctuate.

BARRACKS BRAWL

Whether there's been trouble brewing between platoons or you're just drunk and feel like talking shit to the guy on the catwalk across from you, it's going to go down. Some barracks brawls are an all-out war where blood will be spilled. Some are just a couple of assholes drunkenly screaming at each other in the smoke pit.

BARRACKS BRO

A junior enlisted servicemember you fuck at the end of the night due to desperation.

BARRACKS BUNNY

These subjects are similar to "barracks rats," but generally are females who live in the barracks, belong to the unit, and have their own room at the end of the hall. They love to go room to room riding the dicks of all the men in their platoon until they are more beaten than a girl in an elevator with Ray Rice.

BARRACKS CLEANING

See Field Day.

BARRACKS CUT

Likely the most fucked-up haircut you will get from the "barracks barber."

BARRACKS GOGGLES

The condition where desperation takes over and you just need to fuck something.

BARRACKS LAWYER

Person who has been in trouble so much or been around long enough to think they know how to skate and navigate the UCMJ.

BARRACKS LOVE

When two people from the same barracks date.

BARRACKS MAINTENANCE

When real maintenance crews take forever to show up, some servicemembers try to "Redneck Rig" their own fixes which may or may not make the problem far worse than before.

BARRACKS PARTY

A party at the barracks. Barracks parties can range from a couple of people drinking and watching a movie to an all-out rager that the OOD won't attempt to stop.

BARRACKS RAT

Nasty women who live in your barracks room. They have completely given up on life and survive on the Domino's you ordered, your roommate's beer, and the dicks of everyone in your platoon who dare enter her meat cave.

BARSTOOL COMMANDO

One who talks about their "deployment" from a barstool.

BASIC TRAINING VS. BOOT CAMP

The argument about which training is harder: Army or Marine Corps. Usually includes splitting hairs about exactly how many seconds each one allows you to shower or other dumb shit that won't actually make you a better soldier or Marine.

BASILONE'S JIZZ

Gunnery Sergeant John Basilone's semen. One drop of his glorious nut juice would give you the strength of 20 men, and every woman within sight would run to you asking for just a taste of your man butter.

BAT PHONE

A secondary phone generally used for illicit activities.

BATT BOY

A soldier from the 75th Ranger Regiment.

BATTALION BECKY

A girl who sleeps with everyone in the battalion.

BATTALION BICYCLE

A girl who sleeps with everyone in the battalion.

BATTLE BITCH

Person you order around overseas.

BATTLE BOO

Your best friend during deployment.

BATTLE BUDDY

A partner who travels alongside you, no matter what, and you have each other's backs.

BB STACKERS

Nickname for aviation ordnanceman whose job on the aircraft is to load bombs.

BCG

"Birth Control Glasses," which are the issued prescription glasses in boot camp.

BEANS AND BABY DICKS

Old school MRE that consisted of beans and franks in tomato sauce.

BEANS AND BULLETS

A logistical term for food and ammo.

BEAR

A hairy gay man.

BEARMAT

Range control's call sign at Twentynine Palms.

BEASTING

Doing something with extreme strength. Typically used during workouts or fucking.

BEAT FEET

When you need to get the fuck out of somewhere with extreme haste.

BEAT UP BAG

Someone you like to physically, emotionally or mentally abuse.

BEAT UP BY A GHOST

When you're falling asleep and your head keeps bouncing up and down, making it look like a ghost is punching you in the face.

BEAT YOUR FACE

A command screamed at you when you fuck up and have to do push-ups.

BEAT YOUR MEAT

Masturbating.

BEER DAY

After 45 consecutive days out to sea, a ship is authorized a "Beer Day." Typically, two beers per person. Often the beers are warm just to fuck with your morale.

BEFUCKED

The act of actually fucking so hard that you get confused and experience memory loss.

BEFUCKLE

Intense sex that makes you lose your memory, or you get confused and don't remember what happened or how.

BEG, BORROW, STEAL

The three best ways to acquire a new item. Often you were issued this item already, but someone used this method to acquire it from you.

BEHOOVE

A term used by any form of leadership to sound smart while giving you a condescending suggestion. And possibly the most overused word by SNCOs and brown-nosing NCOs. Typically used when you want to appear intelligent. This is the go-to when addressing your troops about what would benefit them.

BELAY MY LAST

When somebody fumble fucks their words or when they say the wrong thing.

BELL RINGER

Someone who rings the bell during BUD/S training and quits, yet always talks about how they tried out for the SEALs. Usually accompanied by an excuse.

BELOW MY PAY GRADE

When some BOOT brings you a problem that doesn't rate your time or thought and you essentially tell him to fuck off and find someone with less important shit to do to hold his hand.

BELT-FED

Linked ammunition running through a feed-tray into a machine gun.

BELT-FED COCK

Vigorously penetrated by multiple partners in a cyclic fashion. Basically, a gang-bang.

BENNY BOYS

A bunch of gay men.

BERET CHASER

Someone who fucks someone just because they wear a green, tan, maroon, red or gray beret. AKA "Beret Lay."

BERTHING RAT

Same as "Barracks Rat," except on the ship.

BETA CUCKS

Weak, non-military members who like to watch their girlfriends get fucked by dudes with hammer cocks.

BFE

"Butt Fuck Egypt,"
AKA the middle of nowhere.

BFH

"Big Fucking Hammer."

BFO

"Blinding Flash of Obvious."

B-FOP

"Biggest Fucking Head
on Post."

BFR

"Big Fucking Rock."

BFW

"Big Fucking Wrench."

BFYS

"Butt Fuck Your Soul."
To collectively punish a
servicemember until they
want to die.

BIG BERTHA

Big-ass corded impact
wrench with a one-inch hex.

BIG BLUE

A stupid-ass way of
describing the Air Force.

BIG BLUE ARROW

Sending a shoutout or
message via Snapchat.

BIG CHICKEN DINNER

"Bad Conduct Discharge."

BIG DICK BULLET

A round for a
.50 cal machine gun.

BIG DICKIN'

When someone of higher rank
trumps what you're doing.
Usually from a brand new
lieutenant who wants to show
how badass he is, but you end
up losing all respect for him
instead.

BIG FOOT TRACKER

A comedic term to take your
mind off of how poorly the
blue force tracker actually
tracks blue forces.

BIG FUCK OFF

Something irritable because
of its overwhelming presence
or size.

BIG GREEN WEENIE

The term used to describe
anything the Marine Corps or
Army does to fuck you over.

BIG RED

The big-ass red hammer used for aircraft.

BIG RED PIG

U.S. Coast Guard icebreaker.

BILGE DIVER

Sailor who works in the murky, shitty bilges of ships clearing away all the shit built up.

BILGE MONKEY

Same as "Bilge Diver," just more derogatory.

BILLET

The position a servicemember holds that can be used to make you do shit that their rank can't.

BINTANG

Indonesian beer.

BINTANG SWEATS

Hangover sweats from Indonesian rot-gut beer.

BIRD

A much cooler way to say helicopter or jet.

BITCH PLATE

The plate covering the engine of an Abrams Main Battle Tank, held in place mostly by gravity and depression.

BITCHASS

The opposite of a term of endearment. Fighting words.

BITCHING BETTY

The nickname for the alert system on an airplane.

BITE THE SILVER BULLET

When the Doc has to use the "Silver Bullet" thermometer on you to get a rectal temp.

BIVOUAC

Sleeping area while out in the field.

BIVY COVER

A waterproof condom-like covering for the sleeping system.

BLACK CHEVRON MAFIA

Enlisted servicemembers who have each other's backs against the officers who ruin everything.

BLACK FLAG

Flag that signifies the weather conditions are detrimental to your health if you were to PT, which you most certainly will be doing anyways. "You better not fall out either, bitch."

BLACK OPS

Operations carried out with methods that can often be frowned upon, but is sometimes the best way to get shit done.

BLACKHAT

Airborne School instructor who has a tiny penis but compensates by behaving like a giant dick.

BLADE

A sharp thing with an edge rather than a point.

BLANKET PARTY

When you fuck up and your peers take it upon themselves to beat the fuck out of you to teach you a lesson.

BLAST FENCE COUNSELING

Getting whooped by a badass soldier or Marine.

BLASTING ROPE

Slang for ejaculate.

BLAZING

Smoking weed.

BLINKER FLUID

A nonexistent fluid. The term is used to trick new guys into asking where to find the blinker fluid, so they look stupid and get hazed.

BLOOD LOTUS

The imprint a menstruating woman leaves on the sheets.

BLOOD STRIPING

When you achieve the rank of corporal and join the NCO ranks, you also earn the right to wear the blood stripe on your dress blue trousers. As an act of initiation that some pussies might call hazing. Your fellow NCOs beat the ever-loving shit out of your legs with their knees and ensure you won't walk for the next day or two. If you don't receive this treatment, your unit is weak or your peers don't respect you.

BLOOD WINGS

When you graduate Airborne School and they pound the pins from the back of your wings into your chest and make you bleed so you feel cool.

BLOWED UP

Fun way of saying you were hit by an IED.

BLOWJOB FACTORY

One who gives all the blowjobs.

BLUE BALL

The act of fucking without ejaculating until your balls start to hurt.

BLUE BOMBER

Erectile dysfunction pill.

BLUE CANOE

The female form of not coming to climax after stimulation.

BLUE FALCON

"Buddy Fucker." Someone who fucks over their buddies, typically for their own gain. 99% of MPs are top-tier "Blue Falcons."

BLUE FLY

Dude who stands out to females in a negative way.

BLUE FOOTING

When your foot accidentally slides into the sanitation water while you're having sex in the porta-shitter.

BLUE KNEES

A hoe or slut.

BLUE MONEY VALUE BAG

Zipper pouch for cash used during deposits.

BLUE ROCKET

A porta-potty.

BLUE SAUNA

A very hot porta-potty that has been sitting in direct sunlight. You masturbate in these during deployment and coming out to fresh air after is almost as good as the orgasm itself.

BLUE WAFFLE

A beat up pussy with all the diseases. All of them.

BLUEBERRIES

Term for the Navy's blue camouflage that makes you blend into the water and die if you fall in.

BLUEBERRY FUCKSTICK

See "Blueberry" and add "Fuckstick."

BLUEJACKET

An enlisted sailor in the Navy.

BLUF

"Bottom Line Up Front."
Used in emails or messages
to describe what the
correspondence is about.

BMW

"Big Marine Woman."

BOAR PUNCH

The act of getting checked
for STDs. This will happen
to you if you raw-dog a
stripper.

BOAT

Any type of Naval vessel.

BOAT BOO

A sailor's or Marine's
significant other while on
a boat deployment.

BOAT CHUCK

Sailors who are stationed
to a ship.

BOAT DONKEY

Navy personnel who have lived
on an actual ship.

BOAT GOAT

Tucking your penis behind
your legs and bending over.
The tip of the penis must
only have the head revealed,
no shaft.

BOAT HOE

The one sailor everybody
passes around.

BOATSWAINS PUNCH

"Dick Punch." Term used to
haze new guys who arrive at
their first command. Engineers
call it an "HT Punch."

BOB

"Back Office Bitch."

BOBBIN' FOR COCK

When you are exhausted to
the point that you start
falling asleep sitting or
standing up, and as your body
goes back and forth between
conscious and unconscious,
your mouth opens and your
head goes back and forth
imitating the act of sucking
a dick.

BOHICA

"Bend Over, Here
It Comes Again."

BOLO

"Be On The Lookout."

BOMB FARM

Where bombs are kept before
loading on a plane that's
about to take off.

BONERIFIC

Something so outstanding that
it gives you a raging hard-
on. Doesn't even have to be
sexual.

BOOGER EATER

A term used for a not-so-bright servicemember.

BOOGER HOOK

Your trigger finger.

BOOM BOOM ROOM

A usually male client-oriented business wherein any sexual desire can be provided for money.

BOOM STICK

Another term for a rifle.

BOOM TEST

Test conducted by the Air Force to see how long it takes to piss everyone off with sonic booms.

BOONDOCKERS

Ankle-high, safety-steel toe boots.

BOONDOGGLE

A "business" trip to a nice destination in which almost no business is actually conducted.

BOOSTER

A person who steals things, especially automobiles and products from stores.

BOOT

"Barely Out Of Training." Any Marine who has been out of training for less than a year. In combat MOSs especially, one must complete a deployment to rid themselves of that title. Can also be used to describe someone who may not be a BOOT, but is doing some really BOOT shit. In some cases, those people can become "perma-BOOTS" and maintain the title of the lowest scum on earth.

BOOT ASS

An emphasis on how BOOT a BOOT is being.

BOOT BANDS

Elastic bands used to blouse trousers for cammies/utility uniforms. Any gay behavior isn't actually gay if you are wearing boot bands. They also make pretty decent cock rings if you're brave enough.

BOOT BITCH

Not just a BOOT, but a BOOT who is being a special pain in the ass. Possibly crying hazing, a weak body or inept as all hell.

BOOT BLOUSER

Bands used to blouse the bottom of trousers to fit around boots.

BOOT COMMANDERS

See "BootTenant."

BOOT DROP

When a group of BOOTS get to their unit after graduating from their job school and have no idea that their problems are just getting started and that it's gonna be a long night.

BOOT FUCK

A mega BOOT.

BOOTFUCKERY

The actions of brand-new servicemembers who demonstrate just how new and fucking stupid they are.

BOOT LIEUTENANT

A brand new officer who is terrible at just about everything, especially land nav, and is oblivious to how BOOT they are.

BOOT MOVE

An action that demonstrates how new a servicemember is.

BOOT SHARK

A female who preys on new recruits.

BOOT SKATER CHIT

A piece of paper authorizing a recruit to get out of work.

BOOTBITCH

An insult when someone is acting brand-new.

BOOTCAMP FUCKTARD

Kid fresh out of boot camp who thinks he/she knows everything but is still shitting out the food they consumed at the boot camp chow hall.

BOOTENANT

Second lieutenant fresh to his unit who is basically a PFC with way more authority than he should be entrusted with.

BOOTGANISTAN

A theater of operations in which a recruit attempts to become a Marine at MCRD San Diego or Parris Island.

BOOTLICKER

A fucking idiot.

BOOTNECK

A description derived from the Royal Marine commando uniform when they used to cut the top of their boot off and wrap it around their necks to protect them from getting their throats fucking slashed and dying a miserable death.

BOOT-POG-FUCK

Brand-new paper-pushing, non-combat fuck.

BOOTS GONE WILD

A gathering of two or more new servicemembers who are easily preyed upon and always look nervous as fuck. Also, a rare porn video of the hottest PFCs ever documented showing their titties at a barracks party.

BOOTY DUTY

An arrangement where the military member knows they will be getting their fuck on later.

BOPO

"Beat Off, Pass Out."

BORE PUNCH

Where you get your dick swabbed by a corpsman to see if you have an STD.

BOS'N

Head mustang deck department officer. Often the most respected officer at the command.

BOSNIA

A Navy term. "Big Ol' Standard Navy Issued Ass."

BOUNDING

Alternating positions to maneuver on the enemy where one member will support by fire while the other moves to the next location. This will smoke your balls off after 75 meters. You will want to die.

BOX NASTY

A "meal" that is put in a box and shipped to the field when units can't get to the chow hall due to training. Normally consists of a sandwich, granola bar, fruit and disappointment.

BOX OF FREQUENCIES

Fictional radio waves packaged in a box. Often used to trick new guys into looking stupid when they look for the box that doesn't actually exist.

BOX OF GRID SQUARES

An imaginary box of grid squares that keeps BOOTs busy trying to find them.

BRAIN BUCKET

Headgear PPE. You know, like a helmet or something.

BRAIN HOUSING GROUP

Everything inside your skull to include brain, eyes, etc.

BRAIN STRAP

An unnecessary term for a band that holds glasses to the head of the person wearing them.

BRAS

Shooting technique meaning "Breath, Relax, Aim, Squeeze."

BRASS

Shell casings from spent rounds. Can burn the shit out of you when a fresh piece of spent brass flies down your collar, causing you to panic and miss your target or accidentally shoot someone else.

BRAVO ALPHA 11S

Balls.

BRAVO ZULU

Another way of saying "Good Job." Can also be used in a sarcastic manner to tell someone they fucked up.

BREAK IT DOWN BARNEY STYLE

Instructing something as simply as possible.

BRICKS

The barracks. Living quarters for the enlisted.

BRICKS BRAWL

A fight that occurs inside the barracks.

BRIG

Military prison. Servicemembers can be sent there for just about anything.

BROKE

Not working, damaged or destroyed.

BROKE DICK

Someone who is on light duty. Usually, a shitbag who fakes injury to get out of doing work, then becomes a bro-vet when they get out.

BRO-VET

A veteran who lets everybody know he's a vet. His attire usually consists of distressed graphic military t-shirts, cargo pants, combat boots and a high fade. They're usually an asshole who complains his whole enlistment, gets out, then tells people to thank him for his military service.

BROWN BAGGER

A married military member. Someone whose spouse packs them a lunch every day.

BROWN EYE

Butthole.

BROWN NOSER

Someone who sucks up to leadership so hard that their nose is covered in shit from constantly eating the leadership's ass.

BROWN STAR CLUSTER

Dirty, crusty anus.

BROWN THUNDER

Sounds made whilst defecating.

BROWNIES

Navy term used to describe paper towels or any brown paper.

BT PUNCH

A punch to the face from a boiler tech.

BUBBLE GUTS

When out of nowhere your stomach gets pissed off, resulting in rank farts and an immediate need to drop a deuce. Often occurs while on post with no way to address the issue, so you just Kung Fu grip the Hesco barrier and ride the storm until your relief shows up several hours later.

BUBBLEHEAD

A Navy submarine sailor.

BUCK SERGEANT

Newly pinned sergeant. Will mostly likely be on a power-trip in no time.

BUCKET OF YUCK

The best way to describe anybody you find repulsive.

BUD/S

"Basic Underwater Demolition SEAL" is a grueling training course for Navy SEALs said to be the toughest training in the U.S. military. Comes with a guaranteed book deal.

BUDDY FUCKER

Someone who deliberately goes out of their way to get another person in trouble. 100% of military police fall under this category.

BUFF

"Big Ugly Fat Fucker." A term used in the B-52 community.

BUFFALO SWAB

Q-tip for your pee hole when you get swabbed for an STD test.

BUFFER RODEO

Riding on a floor buffer.

BUG JUICE

MRE drink powder. Usually doesn't dissolve evenly, so you go through phases of it being too watered down or too strong. Some theorize that this is intentional in order to keep you guessing so the frustration helps you stay awake while on post.

BUG OUT BAG

A three-day survival pack that, if shit hits the fan, you can grab it and head for the hills. Reserving room for alcohol and porn is highly recommended for trading purposes.

BULKHEAD

A much lengthier way to say wall.

BULL ENSIGN

The most senior ensign (0-1).

BULL PLUG

Engine exhaust cover, typically on jet or turbine engines.

BULLET SPONGE

The person in a platoon who always gets shot. Some units may designate someone as the bullet sponge and send them in first to take all the hits for the rest of the platoon. Usually a BOOT.

BULLWINKLE BADGE

Air assault badge.

BUNKER SHOOT

The female who gets passed around a base inside a war zone.

BURN BAG

Bag of shredded docs that are about to be burned.

BURN THEM

To report something to higher-ups to get someone in serious trouble.

BUTSARGE

Two words rolled into one through a disgruntled sigh. What one says when they've been fucked (extra duty, watch, etc.) by a sergeant before he walks away.

BUTT PUS

Discharge caused by a bacterial infection of the buttocks or anus.

BUTT SHARK

An individual constantly looking for someone to kiss up to. A brown-noser.

BUTTER BAR

The lowest form of self-aggrandizing, knowledge-deficient leadership known to man. Synonymous with dumbass. A second lieutenant who usually flexes that he went to college but is generally still fucking stupid.

BUTTON PUSHERS

People who love getting on your nerves intentionally.

BX/PX BATTLE CRUISER

A fat dependa (military spouse) who roams the BX/PX, normally on an electric scooter. Once they add children they are a BX/PX battle group.

BY THE NUMBERS

Doing things step-by-step in the most tedious way possible.

CABBAGEHEAD

A moron. Person with low intelligence.

CAD-IDIOT

Idiot cadet.

CADILLAC

Mop bucket.

CAGE KICKER

Military corrections officer.

CAKE EATER

A derogatory way to label one as wealthy.

CAMEL CUM

Sweet, thick cream expelled from a camel's testes through his urethra.

CAMEL JOCK

Derogatory term for Middle Easterners.

CAMP WILSON

A small camp on Twentynine Palms where large scale field exercises are based. It includes a chow hall, Warrior Club, PX, laundry room, depression, showers, anxiety and hooches. It beats sleeping outside, but the place still fucking sucks.

CAN OF SQUELCH

Another fake item to tell BOOTs/FNGs to go find, sending them on a wild goose chase while sounding like morons asking for a can of squelch.

CAN'T POLISH SHIT

An expression when a fuck-up is not capable of not fucking up.

CANKED

Cancelled. Can be one of the best words to hear, especially when it's about training you don't want to do.

CANNIBALIZE

When parts are taken from one thing to fix another.

CANNON COCKER

Artilleryman.

CANNON FODDER

Infantrymen who are expendable.

CANOPY LIGHTS

An item new airborne check-ins are sent to find for parachutes.

CAN'T TIE A KNOT, TIE A LOT

The inability to correctly tie a single trusty knot, so instead you just tie about 50 unreliable ones.

CANVAS STRETCHER

A 2-4 person carrier made of canvas.

CAPTAIN JACK

A character in a popular Army cadence.

CAPTAIN'S MAST

Where a CO hands down punishment to a servicemember for possible wrongdoing.

CAR

Combat Action Ribbon, earned from active participation during combat. In some cultures throughout the Marines, if you don't have a CAR, you'll always be a BOOT.

CARL

The guy who always fucks things up and asks stupid questions.

CARPET WALKER

Any MOS in the armed services who is not in the infantry or spends more time walking on office carpet than out in the field.

CASE OF THE ASS

Getting sick.

CAT HOLE

Hole dug in the ground to take a shit in.

CATCH ME, FUCK MES

Marine silkies or other gay short shorts.

CATCHALL

See Article 134.

CATFU

"Completely And Totally Fucked Up."

CAT EYES

Helmet band with patches that light up when viewed through NVGs so you can see each other better at night. People like to write motivational shit on them to feel cool.

CATTYWAMPUS

Not aligned correctly or crooked.

CAVEAT

A caution or warning made in order to make an incompetent person seem smart.

CAW CAW

A servicemember whose body is no longer mission capable. Generally a derogatory term; an insult.

CEM

"Career Ending Move."

CEREBELLUM SHOT

Bullet wound striking the head then passing through the cerebellum.

CHABS

Eight-pack abs. Usually on the douche who takes his shirt off any chance he gets.

CHACH BAG

Wannabe cool guy, usually metrosexual.

CHAIN GANG

A work detail where everyone is lined up and passing materials from A to B. It makes the working party feel sophisticated and looks impressive to leadership.

CHAIN OF COMMAND

The hierarchy of power within the military. The top is always looking for new ways to fuck over the bottom. Your entire experience and opinion of the military for the rest of your life will be determined by the quality of your chain of command.

CHAIR FORCE

A nickname for the Air Force that other branches will use to poke fun at how easy being in the Air Force is, while simultaneously being extremely jealous of how good they have it. Often used by servicemembers who are too dumb to come up with an original joke but still think they're fresh with this one.

CHAIRBORNE

One whose MOS is admin.

CHAIRBORNE RANGER

An enlisted airman who acts high speed, even though he's in the Air Force.

CHALK

A specific aircraft load. Especially a group of airborne soldiers who deploy from a single aircraft.

CHARLIE

Slang for Vietcong. Typically, "Charlie" is everywhere.

CHARLIE BRAVO

Cock-blocker.

CHARLIE DELTA

Cum-dumpster.

CHARLIE FOXTROT

Clusterfuck. When everything has just gone to total shit.

CHARLIE MIKE

Continue mission.

CHARMS

Candy that used to be included in MREs and was considered bad luck by grunts.

CHARTS AND DARTS

The method artillerymen use to calculate shooting arty.

CHECK

See Check Rog.

CHECK FIRE

Order to stop firing for possible error or mis-target.

CHECK ROG

Super cool way to simply say that you understand something.

CHECK VALVE

Air or oil pressure check valve.

CHECK ZERO

To check the zero on your rifle sights to make sure it's actually sighted in. This is usually done because you're not hitting shit and getting made fun of.

CHECKLIST GIRL

When a girl simply goes around the base or barracks and fucks as many dudes as she can to check off her "fuck list."

CHEESE CHARGE

Extra propellant in mortar fire.

CHEESE DICK

A shitbag servicemember who just doesn't give a fuck and is generally pretty lazy.

CHEESE EATER

Brown-noser.

CHEESE KNOCKER

Kiss-ass.

CHEETAH FLIP

When someone freaks the fuck out. Mostly happens with officers and senior enlisted.

CHEETO DICK

Small, dry, crusty penis.

CHEETO ROUNDS

Practice rounds for the MK19 or 203. Upon impact, the round releases orange paint resembling Cheeto dust.

CHEM LIGHT BATTERIES

Another imaginary item used to fuck with the new guys.

CHERRY

Army term for a new guy.

CHERRY-ASS BOOT

A BOOT who just checked into his/her follow on school or to their unit from said school.

CHERRY BITCH

A slightly meaner way to call someone a "cherry."

CHERRY FUCK

An even meaner way to call someone a "cherry."

CHEST CANDY

Medals and ribbons that are usually earned but often just written up for bullshit reasons to make officers feel better about themselves.

CHESTY PULLER

The most decorated Marine in Marine Corps history. A God among Marines. The Man, the Myth, the Legend. Speaking ill of "Chesty Puller" in any way will result in immediate ass-kicking and possible death.

CHEW AND SCREW

To hurry the fuck up and eat, and get back on deck.

CHEWING RUBBER

When you have to do MOPP 4
training for hours.

CHEWY

A more discrete way to say
blow job.

CHICKEN NOODLE HOAGIE

A soup sandwich. A complete
and total mess.

CHICKEN PLATE

Armored SAPI plates that go
in your flak vest unless you
want to risk lightening your
load on a hike and take
them out.

CHICKEN SHACK

Fast-food chicken shop.

CHICKEN VAGINA

A displeasing appearance.
Messy or gross.

CHICKEN WING

When someone is shooting an
M-16 or M-4 and unnecessarily
sticks their elbow way up,
forming what looks like a
chicken wing.

CHIEF

Either a Navy/Coast Guard E7,
or a nickname for a warrant
officer or chief master
sergeant. The rank motivated
sailors wish to obtain.
The rank dirtbag sailors
want to avoid.

CHIEF OF SMOKE

The first sergeant in charge
of a firing battery.

CHIGADERA

Thing.

CHILI MAC MRE

The most-coveted MRE in existence. Fights have broken out over this MRE. We lost a lot of good men over it.

CHINESE FIELD DAY

Taking everything out of a room to clean the room thoroughly. Often done just to fuck with you and totally unnecessary.

CHIPMATE

The way a Filipino sailor says shipmate.

CHOCH BAG

Douchebag.

CHOCH

Douche.

CHODE CAPTAIN

An egomaniacal dickhead with a God complex who gets off on fucking over battle buddies and other servicemembers. Typically captains, but can come from every rank and position.

CHODE SPECKLE

See herpes.

CHOW

Food.

CHOWTARD

An employee with special needs who works at the chow hall.

CHOW HALL

A location where chow is served. If on Camp Pendleton, there is a 100% chance that food is being served by a prisoner.

CHOW HALL BIPOD

A servicemember standing alone in line at the chow hall.

CHOW HOUND

A fat servicemember who only cares about chow.

CHOW-LIBO-PUSSY

CLP. The order of events where a servicemember gets some chow, goes on libo, then finds some pussy.

CHU

"Containerized Housing Unit."

CHU GOBLIN

Female who bangs people inside her CHU.

CHUBBY

A half-boner.

CHUCKLEFUCK

Someone who's fucked up in one way or another.

CHUCKS

"Marine Charlie's" uniform.

CHUMMING

Baiting the water to attract prey.

CIF

"Central Issue Facility." A place where, no matter how hard you scrub your gear, it will never be clean enough.

CIGARETTE ROLL

Empty tube for tobacco.

CIRCLE JERKERS

Those who participate in a circle jerk ritual where multiple men masturbate in a circle. Not gay if there are guns around, you're wearing boot bands, or if it's Thursday.

CIRCULAR FILE CABINET

Trash can.

CIV DIV

Being a 100% civilian.

CIVILIAN

A non-military, or former military member of society.

CLACK CLACK CLACK MAKE SURE CHARLIE DON'T COME BACK

Setting off a claymore on the enemy.

CLAM

Vagina. Often causes you to make poor decisions, but can also get you BAH faster.

CLEAN

A married Marine who lives on base because his wife lives in another city so she's reaping all the benefits of BAH. Not to be confused with a Jody, but she could be a strong contender for that name.

CLEANING DETAIL

A group of junior enlisted in charge of making sure an assigned location is spotless. They will never succeed.

CLEAR AS MUD

When something is completely misunderstood or super unclear. Often happens after an officer spews a bunch of bullshit about a plan but has no idea what he's even talking about.

CLEARED HOT

When a range is about to go live, so death and destruction are about to begin.

CLEARING BARREL

Any warm hole that's good enough to use while you clear your personal chamber but not good enough to date.

CLICK

1000 Meters. Same as a klick.

CLIP

"Calling Line Identification and Presentation."

CLIT TICKLER

See Dick Tickler.

CLOWN OPS

Same as combat operations but involving clowns.

CLP

"Cleaner. Lubricant. Preservative." A lubricant used for cleaning/lubricating weapons. Not recommended for masturbation lube.

CLUSTERFUCK

A grouping of mistakes within a short amount of time, creating one giant fuck-up.

CO

"Commanding Officer." Person in charge of everyone who basically gets paid to fuck shit up so the enlisted can get paid to fix it.

COAST GUARD

The branch of the military that quietly does a bunch of cool shit in the ocean but no one knows about it because they don't talk about it and no one considers them a real branch anyway. The true quiet professionals.

COASTIE

A term for a member of the Coast Guard. Hardly ever used outside the Coast Guard because no one talks about the Coast Guard.

COB

"Close of Business."
End of the workday.
Best time of day.

COCK

"Confirmation Of Combat
Knowledge."

COCK JUGGLER

Someone who juggles cocks,
typically in their mouth.

COCK SALUTER

An enlisted member who sucks
up to officers.

COCK SNIPER

Having precision while
shooting one's own cum load.

COCK SUCK

Someone who sucks up to
everyone in charge of them.

COCK WAFFLE

Another word for jackass.

COCK WARMER

An orifice utilized by junior
Marines or BOOT officers to
say dumb shit out of and also
consume cocks.

COCKASS

Term used to disrespect
a male for being less
intelligent.

COCKBAG

Pouch containing the
testicles only found
on males.

COCKHOLSTER

Refers to a mouth.

COCKING

Pulling the hammer back
until it locks in position.
Preparing a weapon to fire.

COCKPIT

Female pilot or aircrew
who loves to bang.

COCKS AND ROCKS

Lots of dicks and balls.

COCKTRAP

A mouth.

CODE 5 BRAVO

Paramedic radio code
for a shooting.

COLORS

The daily ceremony where the
flags are raised and lowered
on base. Most servicemembers
avoid being outside during
this time so they don't have
to stand at attention and be
slightly inconvenienced.

COMBAT CLIT

Female servicemember in a
hostile environment or combat
theater.

COMBAT COMPANION

Your significant other or friend onsite overseas.

COMBAT JANITOR

Junior enlisted military members who spend the majority of their time cleaning. Usually what most servicemen end up doing at some point.

COMBAT JERK

Jerking off during a firefight or in the middle of intense combat. The excitement is so intense that you don't even need porn.

COMBAT MATTRESS

Female who fucks a lot of dudes and chicks during deployment.

COMBAT NINJA

Top-secret Army MOS, 99 Zulu. They do secret squirrel, badass shit.

COMBAT THONG

Women's tactical panties.

COMMA

Pause for effect.

COMMO

Comms equipment operator.

COMMON SENSE

Uncommon virtue.

COMPANY CLEARING BARREL

A company's number-one hoe. The female who sleeps with all the males.

CONCUR

To agree.

CONER

What bubblehead NUCs call people forward of the reactor on a submarine.

CONE

A conical cylinder, normally orange, used to alert vehicles.

CONN

Conning tower where the ranking officer is in charge of the ship's movements and course.

CONTRABAND

Stuff you're not supposed to have according to the local regulations. Usually traded in basic training.

CONVERTIBLE GO-FASTERS

Vehicles with an amazing ability to become roofless.

CORFAM

High-gloss dress shoe.

CORPS WHORE

Female in the Navy hospital corps who gives out pussy as often as they take vital signs.

CORRECTIVE TRAINING

Training used to set someone straight.

COTDA

"Case Of The Dumb Asses."

COVER

Another military term for a very common item, just to be different. In this case, a hat.

COVER AND ALIGN

The act of getting in a straight line both vertically and horizontally while in formation.

CRACK BARRACKS

The barracks that are in the worst condition.

CRACKING STACKS

Jacking off.

CRANK

Sailor or Marine pulling TAD galley duty.

C-RAT POTATO AND BEEF ENTREE

See C-rats.

C-RATS

A monthly allowance for food given to married military members.

CRAYON

The favorite snack of Marines, grunts and POGs alike.

CRAYON EATER

Marines are stereotypically dumber than a box of rocks, so other branches began calling them "Crayon Eaters." They accepted this nickname while laughing their asses off and wear it with pride.

CRAYON KILLER

Slang for Marine.

CRAYON MUNCHER

A term for Marines who are dumb enough to think crayons are food. Which they are. Blue is the best.

CRIMINAL LANCE CORPORAL

A "Lance Criminal" (E-3) in the Marines who always gets in trouble, or gets away with shit.

CROTCH HUGGER

One who sucks dick or fucks upward in the chain of command.

CROTCH ROT

An untreated STI you picked up overseas and is slowly poisoning your body.

CRUCIAL

A final or very important decision or action. Often used out of context.

CRUMB CATCHER

Mouth.

CRUNCHIE

Tankers and trackers love their grunts, but if your fighting hole is too close to one of their vehicles and they don't see you before taking off, you're bound to get pancaked by those tracks. This is why tankers and trackers refer to their grunts as "crunchies."

CRUNCHY RICE

When a Viet Cong or NVA is run over.

CRUSH DEPTH BUDDIES

Diving partner with whom you'd go all the way to collapse depth.

CRUTCH BRIGADE

Unit of broke dicks who can't deploy due to injury. Many are just faking to get out of deployment but still get a free meal on Veterans Day.

CRYPTO

Cryptologic technician-rated sailors who deal with intelligence gathering.

CRYSACKING

The act of using excuses or trying anything to get out of work or putting forth effort.

CSMO

"Collect Shit and Move Out."

CUCK

Someone who enjoys watching their significant other get fucked by another dude.

CUM BUCKET

Whore.

CUM DUMPSTER

A term used for a total whore whose sole purpose is to be used as a cum receptacle.

CUM TRISCUIT

A Triscuit or cracker that has had semen from multiple people deposited on it.

CUNT

"Civilian Under Naval Training."

CUNT BUBBLE

A labial/vaginal area swollen as the result of suction or heavy rubbing.

CUNT CAP

Garrison cap. Humans call this a "hat" in most cases.

CUNT HAIR

Unit of measurement. About the width of a pubic hair, specifically in the cuntal region.

CUNT MAGGOT

Fly larvae on a rotten vagina.

CUNT NUGGET

An arrogant, stupid asshole.

CUNT PUNCH

Kicking a female right in her snatch.

CURTAIN CALL

Where one is looked over before having to appear in front of the CO.

CUT SLING

When a helicopter releases the load they're carrying by cutting the attachment cable.

CUT SLING LOAD

See Cut Sling.

DA FORM 1

Toilet paper or shit paper.

DAGGON

A substitute for goddamn. No one actually knows what the fuck this means when first sergeant says it.

DAGGON FRIGGEN'

When a first sergeant stutters.

DANGER NOODLE

A Snake.

DARK GREEN

A black Marine.

DARK SIDE

A rank higher than sergeant.

DART

"Dumb Ass Radio Troop."

DAT

"Dumb Ass Tanker."

DAVEY JONES' LOCKER

When something is at the bottom of the ocean.

DAYWALKER

Sgt. Maj. Vines.

DBA

"Doing Business As."

DBAB

"Don't Be A Bitch."

DD-214 MOUNTAINS

The form that grants you your freedom from the military. The most sacred of all parchments. When the admin clerk hands you your glorious DD-214, your days of suffering and misery are finally over. You're truly free. "DD-214 Mountains" are usually reserved for salty E-4s who want to get out and smoke weed.

DEBLOUSE

Taking off the uniform "blouse" (top). Often happens when it's really hot out, when you're part of a working party, or when you lost your cover and need to blend in.

DEAR JOHN

When your girl leaves you for another dude because she can't handle you being away so much, she can't take care of herself, you didn't call her enough when you were in bumfuck nowhere in Afghanistan with no phone, and/or you have PTSD.

DEATH BY POWERPOINT

Endless PowerPoints for "training" that make you feel like death is the only escape. Ironically, this happens often during the suicide prevention training.

DECK

Floor.

DECK APE

A nickname for a BM (boatswain's mate). Meant as a disrespectful term, but since BM is the easiest job in the Navy (ASVAB score 35), they take it as a term of endearment.

DECK PLATE LEADERSHIP

A leadership style where one was brought up from the deck plates to becoming a senior NCO (Chief).

DECONFLICT

Avoiding mishap by coordinating.

DEEBO

When someone strongarms another.

DEEP SEA BUDDY

When two dudes in a submarine get together sexually.

DEFENDER SOCKS

Socks for the security forces defender that are designed with loops in the front for you to grab when you're bent over getting fucked by your chain of command.

DELTA SIERRA

Dipshit.

DENTAL

A mythical place where hungover Marines go after a night of drinking to slime into work at 1200 without looking too, too shitty. It's the one place that gets you out of mandatory anything.

DEPENDAPOTAMUS

A woman who feeds off young
and broke servicemembers.
Often, a fairly large female
these servicemembers will
marry whether it be to get
out of the barracks, their
lack of game, or they just
like 'em big. Usually the
dependapotamus will refuse to
get a job and instead stay
at home either popping out
children that may or may not
belong to her husband, or
spend what little money he
makes on dumb shit online,
like a T-shirt that says
"Marine Wife. Hardest Job in
the Corps."

DEPENDA AMBUSH

A group of dependas joining
together to attack someone by
using their husband's ranks
as leverage.

DEPENDASAURUS REX

See dependapotamus.

DEPLOYMENT 10

A female in the military who
slowly becomes more attractive
the longer you're in the field
or on deployment, and until
she becomes the hottest woman
you've ever laid eyes on. This
phenomenon quickly fades as
you return to civilization and
realize that she is, in fact,
ugly as hell.

DEPLOYMENT CUSHION

A female on a deployment who
gets fucked by everyone.

DEPLOYMENT DODGER

A turd who will do whatever
it takes to get out of going
on a deployment, even if that
"deployment" is a six month
vacation in Okinawa, Japan.
This includes malingering,
actually hurting themselves,
or swallowing every staff and
officer dick in order to get
out of going.

DEPLOYMENT GAY

When it's six months into
deployment and you realize
your buddy has a nice ass.

DEPLOYMENT GOGGLES

The effect known to cause
"Deployment 10s." After being
surrounded by all dudes day-
in and day-out for months
on end, even Caitlin Jenner
would be declared a 10 by
most men on deployment. Can
be used the same way as "Beer
Goggles," except alcohol need
not apply.

DEPLOYMENT HOT

Term used to describe how
much hotter a female is
on deployment compared to
back home. Example, 8-10 on
deployment, 4-6 when back at
home. Also known as, "desert
dime," "desert fox," "desert
goggles," "desert princess,"
and "desert queen."

DEPLOYMENT LOVE

When two servicemembers fall
in love during deployment.
Can be a dangerous time to
fall in love when "Deployment
Goggles" are in full effect.

DEPLOYMENT WIFE

Female you're deployed with
that stands in as your spouse
during deployment.

DEPRESSION

False motivation.

DESERT BODY

Desert deployment fuck buddy.

DESERT DIAMOND

See Deployment Hot.

DESERT DICK

A condition caused by
deploying to the Middle
East wherein the individual
dosen't get to have sex.

DESERT RAT

Another term for desert
deployment fuck buddy.

DESERT ROSE

See Deployment Hot.

DESERT TORTOISE

An endangered desert-dwelling
reptile with a hard shell that
resides on live-fire ranges in
Twentynine Palms, taunting
you to go to prison for
accidentally fucking with it.
Has the ability to shut down
entire ranges and render the
U.S. Marine Corps ineffective
while in its presence.

DESERT YETI

Local females outside base in Twentynine Palms.

DESK DICK

Getting fucked on a desk.

DESK POP

Shooting a pistol at your desk.

DET CORD LOOP

A loop of detonation cord.

DET STACHE

Growing a mustache while on deployment.

DEUCE 1/2 CLUB

A category reached once you have sex inside a large truck known as a deuce 1/2.

DEUCE GEAR

See 782 Gear.

DEVIL

Short for "Devil Dog." Usually used by superiors when addressing their troops, often in a negative way. If you are addressed by this term, you're about to get an ass chewing.

DEVIL BITCH

Female Marine.

DEVIL DOLPHIN

A sailor who's assigned to a Marine unit.

DEVIL DONUT

A Marine whose MOS is military police.

DEVIL DUCK

Same as a "Devil Dog" for a Marine, but for a sailor.

DEVIL'S ANUS

The engine room on the ship.

DEVIL'S NUT

The first orgasm after a period of not having sex.

DFAC

Dining facility. The reason they take out money (BAS) from single soldiers in the military, whether they like it or not.

DICK

"Dedicated Infantry Combat Killer."

DICK BEATER

Hands. For obvious reasons.

DICK BROOM

A mustache so long that while blowing another man, their mustache hairs sweep the dick clean.

DICK BUTT

A character whose body is a penis with the testes forming what looks like his butt, which has a smaller penis and balls coming out of the crack.

DICK CHEESE

The build up of crusty, crystalized sweat on your dick from poor hygiene in the field.

DICK CLOWN

Clown penis or clown dick. An odd shaped penis with a bright red bulbous head.

DICK DANCE

Spinning one's cock in a circle.

DICK DICK GAMES

See Fuck Fuck Games.

DICK DUSTER

A mustache that while sucking on someone's dick would touch the penis and essentially dust it off.

DICKFACE

A derogatory term combining the word dick and face. Could be used to describe someone whose nose resembles a penis, or for a mole or skin tag that looks like a penis.

DICKFUCK

Someone whose behavior warrants two curse words put together.

DICK HOLSTER

See Cock Holster.

DICK KNUCKLE

A useless, non-effective person.

DICK LIPS

A descriptive term to describe soft plump lips that would feel exceptionally good during felatio.

DICK ON MY FOREHEAD

When someone is staring at you like a retard for no reason as if there was a dick attached to your forehead.

DICK PLEASERS

Hands.

DICKSHIT

Combination of calling someone a dick and a piece of shit.

DICK SKINNER

See Dick Beater.

DICK SKINNERS, MOON BEAMS

See Dick Beater.

DICK SKINNERS, SOUP COOLERS

See Dick Beater.

DICK SMITH

Hospital corpsman.

DICK SUCK

Someone who sucks up.

DICK TICKLER

Mustache.

DICK TO ASSHOLE

To get really, really physically close to someone in a very non-sexual way.

DICK TRAP

Mouth.

DICKBAG

Douchebag.

DICKED UP

Something that's totally fucked up and wrong.

DICKNADO

Heli-cockter. When the person with the biggest dick in the platoon spins it around in a circle.

DIDDY BOP

Bouncing up and down while marching. Generally frowned upon and looks pretty dumb.

DIDDY BOPPING

The way P-Diddy was walking out of the courthouse after he beat his court case.

DIE, MOTHERFUCKER, DIE

What machine gunners yell to get the right amount of time on a trigger pull for a machine-gun burst. In a more pussified setting, this can be substituted with "Butter, Butter, Jam."

DIGGER

A combat soldier of the Australian military.

DILDOSER

A monster truck with a dildo on its bumper.

DILIGAF

"Does It Look Like I Give A Fuck?"

DILLY DICK'N

Just another term for fucking around, harmlessly.

DING BAT

Idiot.

DINGUS

Stupid.

DINK

Nickname for the North Vietnamese Army and Viet Cong.

DIP

Necessity in the field. Form of currency during deployments.

DIRKA DIRKA

What *Team American: World Police* taught us people from the Middle East say when talking.

DIRT MERCHANT

An individual who will sell anything.

DIRT NAP

When you smoke a motherfucker and they're laying on the ground dead and it looks like they decided to pass out in the dirt.

DIRT SQUIRREL

A squirrel that manages to stay alive in the desert.

DIRT TURKEY

A chick who bangs a lot of dudes while in the desert.

DIRTBAG

A turd, shitbag, and just generally unmotivated and unreliable person.

DIRTY BIRD

Prostitute.

DIRTY LEG

Everyone not Airborne qualified.

DIRTY NASTY LEG

See Dirty Leg.

DIRTY WIND

Methane gas expelled out of the anus.

DISAPPEAR

Vanish, especially in a shady, get-out-of-shit way.

DISCO BELT

Reflective belt worn on the flight line.

DISGUSTING THING

Term used by drill instructors to insult recruits for doing something "nasty." It's usually not even anything too bad, but fuck you.

DISREGARD

When you say something wrong and want to sound professional while backtracking it.

DITTY

A consistent, easy to memorize saying to help retain information for the process of doing something in the proper order. In boot camp, these sayings are said out loud so instructors know you understand. If you say them outside of training, you'll get made fun of for being a total BOOT.

DITTY BAG

A sailor's laundry bag.

DIVE BOMBING

Jumping into something head first with Kevlar® on for protection.

DNKH

"Damn Near Killed Himself."

DOCKING

Where the head of a circumcised penis is inserted into the tip of another circumcised penis.

DOC

This servicemember is treated like a God amongst the combat arms jobs, especially the infantry. He's probably a little extra fruity, but he'll patch you up when you're fucked up or get you an IV in the barracks when you've drunk yourself into a state of dehydration. If you're still not tracking, he's basically a medic.

DOG AND PONY SHOW

Putting on a show-and-tell for some special visitor or higher-up. It serves no practical purpose. You're going to be bored out of your mind and everyone knows it's bullshit. Truly, the pinnacle of military bureaucratic bullshit.

DOG BONE

When a cock is held horizontally in the mouth with the teeth.

DOG FACE

Nickname for Army infantryman.

DOG LEG

A crooked item.

DOLPHIN BUTTHOLE TIGHT

Tighter than a dolphin's butthole.

DOME

Can mean head in both senses,
either your physical head or
the act of giving/receiving
head (oral sex).

DOME OF OBEDIENCE

Kevlar.®

DONKEY DICK

The attachment for a 5 gallon
fuel jug that acts as a
spout to be able to pour the
contents of the jug into a
fuel port or other small
opening. Resembles the shape
of a large donkey dick.

DONUT LAUNCHER

Ring airfoil grenade launcher
for riot control.

DOOLIE

Freshman at the USAF Academy.

DOPE ON A ROPE

Air-assault soldier.

DORM BUNNY

See Barracks Bunny.

DORM QUEEN

See Barracks Bunny.

DORM RAT

See Barracks Bunny.

DOUBLE DELTA

"Dirty Dick."

DOUBLE DRAGON

Throwing up and shooting
diarrhea out the ass at the
same time.

DOUBLE TIME

Dumbass way to say "run."

DOUBLE UGLY

Nickname for the F4 Phantom II.

DOUCHE CANOE

Obnoxious or despicable person.

DOUGHBOY U.S.

Army soldiers from WWI.

DOWNTIME

No training scheduled.
Free time.

DRAGONFLY WINGS

Air Force airman first class.

DRAHHHP

When a drill instructor or drill sergeant yells for someone to get into the push-up position.

DRIFTWOOD

A boner that goes through the cycle of hard to soft, without you fucking or jerking off, so it's useless and wasted. Also a strip club outside of Camp Lejeune.

DRILL PRIVATE

Usually the platoon guide while you're in basic training. This person relays information or commands from the drill sergeant to the rest of the privates, but also thinks he has some type of power that doesn't exist. Everyone ends up hating him and he probably falls out during training anyway.

DRINKY GIRL

A female at the bar who lets men buy her a ton of drinks without any intention of actually sleeping with any of them.

DRIPPY DICK

See Crotch Rot.

DROP BLOUSE

Taking off your blouse (with rank) to fight someone.

DRUG DEAL

To make a deal for literally anything you need.

DRUNK BUNK

Bar-top dining platform.

DUCK HUNTER

Army Air Defense.

DUE OUTS

Supplies designated to ship out soon.

DUMB STUPID PRIVATE

Self-explanatory.

DUMMY CORD

Standard 550 cord or other apparatus used to attach gear to your body. Usually implemented when your BOOT or platoon dumbass loses something important like his NVGs. Can be used as a preventative measure before he loses it because, let's face it, without that shit tied to him, he's going to lose it.

DUNE COONS

Derogatory term for terrorists in the Middle East.

DUSTOFF

"Dedicated Unhesitating Service
To Our Fighting Forces."
Sometimes called a medevac.

DUTCH OVEN

Where one farts in the covers
and throws the blanket over
them so they suffer from the
smell.

DUTY BITCH

One who is on watch and
usually does tasks that no
one else wants to fuck with.

E-TYPE

Enlisted-type.
Also known as E-Dogs.

E.A.D.A.D.Q

"Eat a Dick and Die Quick."

E-3 1/2

Having picked up, but not
pinned, E-4. Also known
as a senior lance corporal
in the Marines.

EAGLE DRIVER

F-15 pilot.

EAGLE HATCHER

Member of the F-15
development team.

EAGLE KEEPER

F-15 maintainer crew chief.

EAGLE RIDER

F-15E weapons system officer.

EAR PRO

Ear protection. Whether it's faulty earplugs that result in a massive class-action lawsuit four years down the road, or the cigarette butts you policed earlier, something is better than nothing when you're in loud environments. If you're in real combat, you ditch that shit and hope for the best. But it's required for training because "we train like we fight" or some shit.

EAT BABIES

A term created due to being called "baby killers" by hippies upon return from Vietnam.

EATING DUCK

Eating quickly.

EBD

"Explosive Bloody Diarrhea."

EBS

"Exploding Butt Syndrome." It's when you think and hope it's just a fart but there's also a really good chance you might shit yourself.

EDL

"Equipment Distribution List." Serialized gear (rifle, optics, NVGs, IR lasers, flares, etc.) that needs to be accounted for, as it cannot be replaced and can cause harm to your unit. Heart attacks happen when you realize your NVGs aren't in your NVG pouch.

ERRONEOUS

Any E-7s who want to sound smart. Also see Behoove.

EIGHT UP

Something shitty. See 8 Up.

EMBRACE THE SUCK

When the task you're currently undertaking is going to suck a bag of baby dick but someone has to do it, and that sorry asshole is you, so you just have to accept it and keep pushing.

EMERALD SHELLBACK

One who crossed the Greenwich line and equator on a ship.

EMI

"Extra Military Instruction." See Hip Pocket Class or Hazing.

ENDEX

"End of Exercise." Commonly mistaken for "index." The sweet word that means you're done running around in a full kit in triple digit heat, at least for now.

E-NOTHING

E-3 and below in rank. Non-NCO. Also see BOOT or "Cherry."

ERR

A way to communicate your understanding of information being passed. Usually a sarcastic response lacking in motivation. The typical response of the terminal lance who couldn't give any less of a fuck.

ERRAHH

Noise a Marine makes when responding to proper greeting, or showing an increased enthusiasm for something.

ETADIK

A fictional pill for someone to take when they need to eat a dick.

ETHOS WARRIOR

Better known as the "Soldier's Creed," is a motivational pledge to defend the country. All Army personnel are required to memorize and repeat it out loud, every day, during morning formation.

E-TOOL KILL

Getting a kill by beating the enemy to death with your issued e-tool/ folding shovel. Absolutely barbaric and bonerific.

EVERY SWINGIN' DICK

When absolutely every single motherfucker needs to be involved in something.

EXHAUST SAMPLE

The process involves taking a trash bag and holding it over the exhaust port while someone else revs the vehicle and black diesel smoke goes everywhere but inside the bag. If done wrong, you'll end up with burning eyes and hacking up a lung after you've inhaled a hazardous amount of exhaust fumes. Whoops.

EYEBALLS

A term used by drill instructors to get the recruits to look at them.

FACE FUCKED

When you repeatedly gag someone with your cock. Humping someone's face and forcing your dick down their throat.

FACEBOOK WARRIOR

Someone who flexes how tough they are on Facebook even if they have never served a day in the military.

FAG

"Fresh Ass Grunt."

FAG BAG

Flight suit.

FAG STRAP

A sling worn after an arm injury.

FAN ROOM COUNSELING

The Navy version of Wood-Line Counseling, where someone is taken to a discrete location to punished them without supervision.

FANG

"Fucking Air National Guard."

FANGBRUSH

Toothbrush.

FANTAIL PHANTOM

The mysterious sailor or Marine who shits off the fantail.

FAP

A servicemember's favorite pastime. Plain and simple: it's beating your dick like it owes you money. Maybe you're horny, maybe you're depressed, or maybe you're just bored as fuck and need something to pass the time.

FAP TENT

A quick and easy shack made for the purpose of beating your meat. Usually made out of your poncho and some 550 cord.

FAPPED OUT

When you get sent to the Fleet Assistance Program and are given a task away from your normal unit to help around base. This is usually a good thing so you can get away from your damn unit. You might land in a unit that actually cares about you. Sure, you might be doing a dumb job, but it's better than being with your unit.

FARMER ARMOR

Improvised vehicle armor. Highly popular in the early days of Operation Iraqi Freedom.

FART BAG

Sleeping bag/system.

FART BOX

A derogatory term for a girl's (or dude's) asshole. Generally one that you are interested in penetrating.

FART CART

Auxiliary ground air-pressure unit to start certain jets.

FART SACK

Flight suit.

FAST

"Fake-Ass SEAL Team."

FAST MOVERS

A childish way of saying something. In this case: jets.

FAT BODY

The big boys of the military. They'll have burgers or pizza for every meal, skip PT, but it's all good because "it's just a thyroid problem."

FATAL FUNNEL

The doorway where you are most likely to be killed when you enter a room to clear it of assholes.

FATIGUES

Duty/work uniform.

FAYETTEVILLE FINE

A person who is only hot in the Fayetteville area.

FERDA

"For the."

FIDDLE FUCKING

Goofing off.

FIDO

"Fuck It, Drive On."

FIELD BOOTY

Getting laid while training in the field.

FIELD DAY

A weekly ritual where you clean your workspace and barracks room to unnecessary levels. The newer you are, the more painful field day is going to be. There's no way to win field day. It's not so much about how clean your room is as it is about who's inspecting and how big of a douche they are.

FIELD EXPEDIENT

Doing something quickly and efficiently.

FIELD FUCK

See Field Booty.

FIELD GOGGLES

See Deployment Goggles.

FIELD JACKS

Jerking off in the field.

FIELD JERK

Beating off in the field. Possibly hidden or possibly on-post with your buddy because neither of you give a shit.

FIELD LOVE

See Field Booty.

FIELD MATTRESS

Sleeping mat that rolls up and attaches to your ruck.

FIELD SHOWERS

A makeshift shower done while training in the field. Usually consists of baby wipes or canteens of water.

FIELD SNATCH

See Field Booty.

FIELD WIFE

The girl you always hang out with or fuck during a bivouac. This can also be a new guy that you make do chores for you.

FI-FI

Improvised pocket pussy made from MRE bags and peanut butter/cheese spread. A latex glove with lotion inside that you jack off with.

FIGJAM

"Fuck I'm Great, Just Ask Me."

FIGMO

"Fuck It I Got My Orders."

FILIPINO MAFIA

Anyone of Filipino descent. Primarily Navy and stationed in California/West Coast/ FDNF Japan. Also primarily "supply" rates. Advances way ahead of peers if upper leadership is part of the Mafia.

FINE LINE BETWEEN HARD & RETARD

Where one's actions are so extreme it's gonna be swayed one way or the other.

FINGER FUCK

To use ones fingers to get deep inside of crevices for cleaning purposes.

FINGER FUCK IT

See Finger Fuck.

FIRE WATCH READING MATERIAL

Writing that has terrible content, but you read it to pass time on fire watch.

FIREFLY

Where something is working but is in bad shape.

FIREWATCH

A roving post set up during downtime to ensure safety of the area, and apparently to make sure no one catches on fire for some reason.

FIREWATCH RIBBON

The National Defense Ribbon everyone used to get by default for finishing boot camp, basically learning how to stand firewatch.

FIRST SARTENANT

A cross between a first sergeant and a lieutenant.

FIRST SAUSAGES

Nickname for first sergeant.

FISH

"Fuck It, Shit Happens."

FIST

"Fucking Idiot Searching for a Target."

FISTER

Fire-support team member.

FISTERING

When two guys are carrying something heavy and you put two fingers on the object as they pass so you can say that you helped.

FITFO

"Figure It The Fuck Out."

FIVE-FINGER DISCOUNT

See Tactically Acquire.

FIVE JUMP CHUMP

One who has just graduated Airborne School.

FIXING STUPID

Fixing a person who is stupid.

FLAMING ASSHOLE

A jet's afterburner during combat operations.

FLAT BLACK

Black paint with no gloss. Typically used for tactically spray-painting dicks on things.

FLAY

Peel the skin off a corpse with a knife.

FLEET DODGER

A person who avoids deployments and any MOS that requires them to spend more than one week per year in the field.

FLIGHTLINE

Where aircraft are parked and worked on.

FLOB

"Free-Loading Oxygen Breather."

FLUX CAPACITOR

The part that's broken when the new lieutenant asks what the problem is.

FM

"Fucking Magic."

FNG

"Fucking New Guy."

FOAD

"Fuck Off And Die."

FOB

"Forward Operating Base." The levels of shittiness will vary, but the living conditions are usually pretty shitty throughout.

FOB 10

See Deployment 10 or Field 10.

FOBGOBLIN

Chick on the FOB who's a slut.

FOBBIT

When you aren't fortunate enough to actually leave the FOB, so you end up spending your whole deployment there.

FOD

"Foreign Object Damage."

FOOD BLISTER

Fat body.

FOOTBALL BAT

Something or someone who is very jacked up beyond the norm.

FORCED HYDRATION

Where one is forced to drink water due to fear of dehydration.

FORESKIN

Issued neck gator that's used for warmth or to keep dirt out of your face.

FORWARD

Moving to the direction at the front of the formation. Pretty self-explanatory, but that's the military for you.

FOUR AND OUT

When you just do your four years then EAS/ETS, because you realized reenlisting would be a terrible idea.

FOUR POINTS OF CONTACT

Holding onto a surface with both feet and hands touching the surface at all times.

FOX DEUCE

See Face Fuck.

FOXTAIL

Military name for a bench brush. Not to be confused with a foxtail buttplug.

FRAG-O

Fragmentary order.

FREAKIN' DAMN

A more fun and intense way to say damn.

FREEDOM BIRD

Airplane ride home after deployment. Likely to stop in Ireland so you get a strong buzz going before departing again, then everyone has to piss, but the seatbelt sign is still on so it becomes a huge clusterfuck and staff sergeant yells at everyone.

FREEDOM BONER

When you and your buddies are blowing shit up, shooting machine guns, and just generally "getting some," and the experience produces such elation that you get a metaphoric hard-on for how hard you are freedoming.

FRESH NUTS

Clean testes.

FRESH SOCKS

Putting new socks on after a long day in the field.

FRESH WATER JELLYFISH

When someone ejaculates in the shower but it doesn't go fully down the drain so it just sits there and looks like a jellyfish.

FRICKEN

A way to say "fucking" politely.

FRIENDLY-FUCK

Taking fire from a friendly unit. Sometimes intentionally because that piece of shit sergeant just has to go.

FRIGGIN' DOGGON' TRASH

When a SNCO is talking about a shitty person or equipment.

FRIG'N

A slightly different way to politely say "fucking."

FROG HOG

Women who specifically try to fuck Navy SEALs.

FROGMAN

Navy SEAL nickname.

FROGS

Navy SEAL nickname.

FROMUNDA CHEESE

Cheese-like substance from under the balls to your taint.

FRONT LEANING REST

Push-up position.

FRUIT LOOP

Someone who's gay. Usually in the Navy.

FRUIT SALAD

One who has a lot of medals and ribbons on their dress uniform.

FTA

"Fuck The Army."

FTMC

"Fuck The Marine Corps."

FTN

"Fuck The Navy."

FUBAR

"Fucked Up Beyond All Recognition."

FUBIJAR

"Fuck You Bitch, I'm Just A Reservist."

FUCK

Most universal word in the military dictionary that can replace any word in any language.

FUCK A DUCK

A phrase meaning you stopped truly giving a fuck.

FUCK BOI

Douchebag who tries to fuck and fuck-over chicks.

FUCK BUDDY

Person you fuck on a whim with no strings attached.

FUCK FACE

Someone who is fucking up or is incompetent.

FUCK FUCK GAMES

Punishment that involves useless games that have no training value and only serve to destroy morale and increase the chances that your troops want to murder you before they kill themselves.

FUCKHEAD

Someone who's being a dumbass.

FUCK KNUCKLE

Someone who's being difficult.

FUCK-ME FRIDAY

A Friday where nothing goes your way and you keep getting fucked over.

FUCK ME SIDEWAYS

A sense of disbelief.

FUCKMOTHER

A mother who wants to fuck you, spoil you and buy you stuff.

FUCKNUGGET

A person with a low IQ.

FUCKNUTS

Multiple idiots together in a group.

FUCK PIG

An ugly person you fuck just for fun.

FUCK PUPPET

Someone you brutally fuck without concern for their safety.

FUCK-START

Pull-starting or push-starting with your cock.

FUCKSTICK

A stupid person who is usually lower ranking than the person yelling at them.

FUCK TENT

A tent you fuck in.

FUCK THIS

A way to express the disdain you have for a particular situation.

FUCK TON

A unit of measure. Very heavy.

FUCK TROPHY

Offspring.

FUCK WAGON

The way douchebags describe their ride to make you think they actually fuck in it.

FUCK YOUR HAT

A solution to not being able to fuck your woman due to circumstances that are not in your control.

FUCK, MARRY, KILL

A game usually played by servicemembers when they're bored where one must decide to fuck one, marry one or kill one. You have three choices.

FUCKCHOPS

Sideburns so sexy you're bound to get laid.

FUCKED

Completely screwed.
No way to fix the situation.

FUCKED THE DOG.
SCREWED THE POOCH.

When someone screws up or drops the ball on something.

FUCKEN CHOCH

A douchebag.

FUCKENING

When the chain of command ruins your day with some bullshit comment or dumbass tasking.

FUCKER

A gender-neutral term usually said between friends about that guy you really don't fucking like.

FUCKERY

Similar to skating, but doing riskier shit and not being sneaky enough about it.

FUCKIN' LEG

Non-Airborne personnel.

FUCKIN' SOUP SANDWICH

Something that's a total mess. Kind of like an original soup sandwich, but with a double serving of fuckin'.

FUCKING FUCK FUCK

Extreme fuck. Twice as bad.

FUCKING GODDAMN

The use of goddamn with the pretense of fucking. Used often by drill instructors as a lead-in to referencing any object.

FUCKINGDAMN

Used as a filler, mostly by staff NCOs, when they lose their train of thought during a period of instruction, passing of word, or an ass-chewing.

FUCKINNNNNNNNNNN'

An expression used to stall while thinking of the correct thing to say.

FUCKLE

When you kiss your girl whilst penetrating her with your dick.

FUCKO

Common greeting for someone you don't like.

FUCKSHIT

When you want to call someone a fucker and a shithead.

FUCKSTART YOUR FACE

The act of violently using your penis to force into in the other persons mouth with the intent to harm.

FUCKSTICK, DICK SKINNER

An idiot who is assumed to be jacking off.

FUCKTARD

Just another insult.

FUCKTASTIC

Fanfuckingtastic.
Also, very fantastic.

FUCKY

Something that is wrong
or odd.

FUEL FARM

Where vehicles and tankers
get fuel.

FUCK TANGLE

A really bad knot in your
550 cord.

FUGLY

Fucking ugly.

FULL ANAL NELSON

Putting a girl in the full
nelson while fucking her ass.

FULL BATTLE RATTLE

Having all of your gear on.

FULL BIRD PRIVATE

Nickname for Army and Navy
enlisted rank of E-4, due
to the bird on the rank.
Kind of like a colonel, but
not even close.

FULL BUCKET OF CHICKEN

A fat person.

FULL SEMI-AUTO

Burst fire or three-round
burst. Sometimes used by CNN
to describe how Glock-15s
shoot.

FULL SEND

The act of doing something
reckless just for the fuck
of it. YOLO.

FUN BOX

Vagina.

FUN RUN

Long runs that are not fun.
Usually intended to boost
morale, but actually does the
opposite.

FUN POLICE

Anyone in a leadership
position who likes to
squash morale for their own
amusement, or they're just
suffering from a power trip.

FUNGUS

"Fuck You New Guy. You Suck."

FUPA POUCH

Extra fat below a woman's
belly button surrounding
the pelvic area creating an
upside-down triangle of fat.

FUZZY

A brand new private in the
Army who has no rank yet,
so he/she just has the fuzzy
part where a rank patch is
supposed to go.

GAF

"Gay As Fuck."

GAFFING OFF

Not paying attention.

GAGGLE

Loose formation of confederates, primarily E-3 and below, that may or may not be plotting a coup of some kind.

GAGGLE FUCK

A group of people with no sense of uniformity and no rhyme or reason for anything they're doing.

GAMING THE GAME

NBA betting scandal.

GANAHERPASYPHIAIDS

Gonorrhea, herpes, syphilis, and AIDS all at the same time.

GANGWAY

Usually a Navy term that basically means "get the fuck out of my way," but the Marines started saying it for some reason, too.

GARBAGE SAUCE

The opposite of awesome sauce, referring to something that's really bad.

GASTRO

The sickness you get on the ship when you shit and throw up at the same time.

GAT

Another term for "gun" that makes you feel a little more gangster, but also disconnects you from the military world for a split second, which is always a good thing.

GATOR

Nickname for an interrogator.

GATOR ROLL

When you're masturbating and someone walks in so you roll over real fast.

GAUNTLET

Although there are many examples, the Marine Corps has an unofficial hazing ceremony of newly-promoted NCOs to earn their blood stripe by getting kneed in the legs 'til they are black and blue.

GAY

Where one is or isn't homosexual. It can be very complicated, and therefore also means that something is dumb.

GEAR QUEER

Someone who collects military gear. Often someone who isn't even infantry, has no idea how to use it, and still has the tags on shit.

GAY CHICKEN

A contest of willpower, determination, pride, and comfort in your sexual orientation. The goal is to get as gay with your opponent as possible until one of you taps out. "Gay Chicken" is known to get taken to extreme levels when played by infantrymen after being stuck on ship or on deployment for extended periods of time.

GAY DONUT

Someone's butthole.

GAYZER

See Pecker Checker.

GEAR ADRIFT IS A GIFT

When you find some gear that is unsecured and unguarded. That gear just became your gear, whether you need it or not.

GEAR BOMB

A massive pile of everyone's gear together which will make it impossible to distinguish whose gear is whose unless you have adequately marked yours beforehand. This is the prime time for gear thieves.

GEARDO

See Gear Queer.

GEEDUNK

The unit snack bar. Not to be confused with Aloha Snackbar.

GEEDUNK BANDIT

The person that will always "fly" if you "buy".

GENIUS

Where one is called this and actually is, or someone who did something dumb.

GEOBACHELOR

Servicemembers who are married but for one reason or another elect to live in the barracks instead of with their own family.

GET FUCKED

When someone is going to have to deal with something that no one wants to but you feel no sympathy for them and let them know that you know they are going to hate life and you don't give a fuck.

GET HOT

Get moving.

GET SMOKED

Getting killed.

GET SOME

Killing or stacking bodies.

GETTING A PURPLE HEART

Getting punched on the heart by the sergeant major.

GETTING HEMMED UP

When you are doing some acting a fool, and you get caught by someone who isn't going to let it slide.

GETTING SMOKED

Physical exercise used as a punishment for a fuck-up.

GHOST TURD

Lint from clothing that falls onto the floor.

GI GIN

Barracks or field cocktail.

GI PARTY

Barracks cleanup.

GIB

"Guy In Back."

GIG LINE

The invisible vertical line from the trouser button to the edge of the belt and to the buttons on a service shirt. Don't fuck it up.

GIGGLE JUICE

Alcohol.

GIVE 'EM ONE

When someone does something that deserves recognition. The Marine talking about said person says, "Give 'em one." All Marines in attendance will sound off with "Kill!"

GLASS SLIPPERS

Hooker shoes.

GLORY HOLE

Magic hole in a stall where one can get a random blow job.

GLOW WORMS

People who worked in HAZMAT.

GOAT LOCKER

Room for chiefs, senior chiefs and master chiefs to conduct "chief business."

GOAT FUCKER

A nickname for Middle Eastern men.

GOATFUKISTAN

Another name for Afghanistan.

GOBI

"General Officer, Bright Idea."

GODSPEED

To wish someone well.

GOFASTERS

Childish term for the running shoes you recieve at boot camp.

GOFO

"Grasp Of Fucking Obvious."

GOLDEN SHELLBACK

One who crosses the equator at the International Date Line.

GOMOR

"General Officer Memorandum Of Reprimand."

GOOD COOKIE

Good Conduct Medal. Awarded to people who didn't get caught fucking up.

GOOD ENOUGH FOR GOVERNMENT WORK

When you are putting out subpar work but government work is shitty and you're a federal employee so, fuck it, it's good enough.

GOOD IDEA FAIRY

The "Good Idea Fairy" is a sadistic creature that sits on the shoulders of staff NCOs and officers, and feeds them the most insufferable and pointless ideas for their troops to endure.

GOOD TRAINING

Any type of training that doesn't result in anyone being hurt or killed.

GOOD TRASH

When something is good.

GOOK

Term for a North Vietnamese or Viet Cong soldier.

GOON

Someone who's a moron.

GORILLA FIST

To use brute force when a deft touch is needed.

GOUGE

Information put out, typically by an officer.

GRAB ASS

General horseplay and fucking around with your buddies, usually because you are standing by to stand by to stand by some more with no end in sight.

GRAB SOME REAL ESTATE

Area to do push-ups and other ground exercises.

GRAPE

Dumb word for someone's head.

GREASE MONKEY

Wrench-turner, maintenance person.

GREAT TRAINING

A sarcastic phrase used to describe really shitty training. Officers are usually oblivious to the sarcasm.

GREEN BEAN

One of the most magical coffee shops in the Middle East. Hands down better than Starbucks.

GREEN DOT / RED DOT

Sight for a rifle.

GREEN MATTRESS

Someone who gets fucked by Task Force Green dudes.

GREEN MONSTER

The large green knowledge book that recruits at Marine Corps boot camp take with them everywhere.

GREEN TIP

Standard issue M855 5.56mm ammo that has a green tip.

GREEN WEENIE

The military experience. It's a never-ending fuck-fest where you're bent over and taking it whether you like it or not. You signed on the dotted line and it's time to pay for it.

GRENADE

Fat bitch.

GRINDER

Courtyard where one practices marching.

GROTOPOTAMUS

A subspecies locally found near Groton, CT, home of the Navy's Enlisted Submariner School.

GROUND POUNDER

Infantrymen who pound the ground with their feet as they hump, patrol and walk everywhere they go. It is an unfavorable and unforgiving mode of transportation.

GROUND SHEET

Chick who sleeps around.

GRUNT

Infantryman.

GRUNT WORK

Absolute shit work that no one wants to do, so you might as well throw some grunts at it since they're probably just standing by anyway.

GTFO

"Get The Fuck Out."

GUCCI

When something is all good.

GUCCI GEAR

Expensive gear that's typically not needed.

GUCKLE

Storage space in a submarine. Gumshoe cryptologic technician-rated sailor.

GUMBI

Flexible.

GUN BUNNY

An attractive female who uses her body to get attention on social media by posing with guns and gear made for ops she would never go on.

GUN DECK

Navy term to fabricate or falsify qualifications.

GUN ROCK

Artillery crewman.

GUNNY PUFFER

One who fucks or sucks up to gunny to get treated better.

GUNNY TIME

Where gunny does a sidebar after formation and makes a speech.

GUNS UP

A saying amongst Marine Corps machine gunners (0331s) that refers to the act of getting your machine gun up, running, and on target lay down some belt-fed hate downrange.

GUT SLUT

Ladies who run the gut trucks.

GUT TRUCK

Shitty food truck with a C-rating that is more than likely owned by a retiree who parks outside the unit spaces for lunch.

GYNAHERPACYPHILLITIS

A made-up medical term used to describe what you could possibly contract if you have sex with the local stipper off-base.

H&S COMPANY

"Headquarters and Service Company." The conglomeration of POGs who help run each battalion, from admins and supply to motor transport and maintenance personnel. They are characterized by almost always getting off work by 1630, having two-hour chow times, and getting awards for doing their jobs.

HABU

"Hook A Brotha Up."

HAHO

"High-Altitude, High-Opening."

HAJI

Middle East people, mostly terrorists.

HALO

"High Altitude Low Opening."

HAMMERED DOG SHIT

Just how dumb privates and lieutenants can actually be.

HANGAR QUEEN

An aircraft that is always down for maintenance.

HANO

See HAHO and HALO.

HAPPY SOCK

Sock that one jacks off into.

HARD CHARGER

One who is motivated.

HARDER THAN WOODPECKER LIPS

When your dick is very hard.

HATCH

Door.

HAWK

Extreme cold weather.

HAZING

The act of fucking with the new guys because it happened to you and now it's your turn to be the asshole. It has the power to turn shitbags into squared away troops and squared away troops into shitbags, so use it wisely.

HEAD

Restroom.

HEALTH AND WELFARE/COMFORT

Where the chain of command gets the master room key and randomly searches your room for contraband in an attempt to burn you for every little fucking thing for their enjoyment while claiming it's for your health and comfort.

HEAT CAT TOWEL

Towel folded just where your balls are noticeable.

HEINOUS

A word used by higher-ups and drill instructors to over-exaggerate just how bad a minor infraction is.

HELICOPTER KEYS

Keys that don't exist for a helicopter that does.

HERC DOC

C-130 troubleshooter maintainer.

HERDING CATS

Trying to keep a lot of BOOTs in-line or on task.

HERO

Over-motivated person.

HERPA DERP

When someone makes a dumbass decision that everyone knew would go terribly wrong. Typically done by an officer.

HEY DEVIL/SHIPMATE/SOLDIER/ JOE/WINGMAN

A term SNCOs use to address fucked up people they don't know or whose name they don't remember because they don't really care about them and just need to get their attention to chew them out.

HEY JOE

A way to express how fucked up the situation or group of people are.

HICKEY OFF BULKHEAD REMOVER

Bilge cleaner.

HIGH AND STUPID

When a haircut is higher than high and tight.

HIGH AND TIGHT

Haircuts for the most BOOT and motivated individuals. Consists of shaving the sides of the head and only leaving hair on the top of the head. They look ridiculous and are sure to ID you as a BOOT-ass bitch or motard.

HIGH AND TO THE RIGHT

Literally, when your shot at the rifle range is high and to the right but has been repurposed to mean that you missed your shot at anything in life.

HIGH SPEED

Someone or something that is highly advanced at what they do. Also know as, "high-speed, low-drag."

HIGH TECH PIECE OF TRASH

High-tech equipment that's really just expensive garbage.

HIJAB

Female Muslim head dress.

HILLBILLY ARMOR

See Farmer Armor.

HIP POCKET

Extra training after the scheduled training is finished.

HIP POCKET CLASS

Usually short classes on unimportant knowledge that will never be used just to kill time.

HIT THE SILK

The act of ejecting from an aircraft and parachuting down.

HMC

Hospital corpsman chief.

HMFIC

"Head Motherfucker In Charge".

HOFNR

Pronounced HAWF-NER; acronym for "Hard-On For No Reason."

HOG

"Hunter Of Gunmen." Sniper with a kill.

HOG HUNTING

See Hogging.

HOGGING

Planning on going out with the intent of fucking a fatty.

HOLIDAY FLAG

Special giant flag used for holidays.

HOLLYWOOD MARINE

Marine who went through MCRD in San Diego. Parris Island Marines like to make fun of them for whatever reason.

HOOAH

Cheesedick way to say you understand something. Also something that junior enlisted say to NCOs and officers when they want to say "Fuck you" but not get a counseling statement.

HOOKER BAG

Condom.

HOOKING AND JABBING

Fightin' and shit.

HOOVER

Engine noise the S-3 and A-10 make.

HOOYAH

Navy version of "hooah" or "oorah" to show understanding, motivation, or fake motivation.

HORSE COCK

Dude with a huge dick.

HORSE MARINE

A Marine from rural America. They wear 10-gallon hats, dip Grizzly, wear shit-kickers, and always stink like shit.

HOT DOG DOWN A HALLWAY

The state of a girl's genitals after she gets a train ran on her at the barracks and she is so loose that you could get lost in there.

HOT GARBAGE

A shitty servicemember.

HOT MINUTE

In a while.

HOT RACK

On a submarine, sailors somewhat share racks so while one is working, the other is sleeping.

HOTBOXING

Where one farts next to someone in the same car and locks the windows.

HOTTER THAN TWO MICE FUCKING IN A WOOL SOCK

An expression used to describe how ridiculously hot it is.

HOUSE MOUSE

A small recruit who acts as the drill instructor's personal bitch.

HOUSEHOLD 6

Call sign for a military spouse.

HOWEVER COMMA

Used when you have stated something and have to put in an exception because someone is that stupid (an E-nothing) and can't figure it out on their own.

HUA

"Head Up Ass."

HUGA

"Heard. Understood. Go Away."

HUMP

The most common method of transportation for the infantry. Hiking with all the gear they will need for whatever mission they are conducting and probably a bunch of extra shit that is totally unnecessary.

HUMVEE KEYS

Another imaginary item that exists as a great way to fuck with new people.

HURRICANE PARTY

A party in the barracks during a hurricane when the base is on lockdown.

HURRY UP AND WAIT

The military's way to make sure no one is late but everything goes at snail sperm speed.

HYDRATE

A more scientific way to say drink water.

HYDRATE OR DIE

Drink water or die of dehydration.

I'LL FIGHT FOR YOU

The phrase your leadership says when they want you to think they care about your needs but really don't give AF.

ICE CREAM SOCIAL

Rare time on a ship where there is ice cream and karaoke in the galley for "morale." Usually followed by bad news the next day.

ID-10T CERTIFIED

When someone is an idiot.

ID-10T FORM

The imaginary "idiot" form BOOTs are told to find when they are being fucked with.

IED HOPSCOTCH

Where one moves down an IED-filled path little-by-little.

IF IT MOVES, SHOOT IT.
IF IT DOESN'T MOVE, PAINT IT.

JTAC/CCT sayings.

IF YA AIN'T CHEATIN', YA AIN'T TRYIN'

Where one cheats to finish something or best someone and doesn't get caught.

IF YOU CAN'T TRUCK IT, FUCK IT.

Motor T phrase meaning things that are unable to be hauled by them are irrelevant.

IHTFP

"I Hate This Fucking Place."

I'LL JUST GO FUCK MYSELF

When someone angrily separates themselves from a situation or conversation.

IN CADENCE

To do something like marching or PT in unison.

IN COUNTRY

One being in a foreign country or territory.

IN LIEU OF

A more complicated way of saying "instead of."

INDOOR PT

Physical training that the fair-weather Air Force conducts.

INFIDEL

What Jihadis call westerners or enemies.

INK STICK

Another unnecessary way to say the name of a simple object. In this case: pen.

INSTALLATION BEAUTIFICATION

Cleaning up the base or unit spaces.

INSTRUMENTAL

Something or someone of importance.

INTESTINAL FORTITUDE

Where one has balls.

IRON DUCK

Someone who can't swim.

IRON RAIN

Massive invasion force.

IRISH PENNANT

Loose or frayed material hanging off of an article of clothing. Something so small can make a big impact on the quality of your day if you have one during a uniform inspection.

IRREGARDLESS

A made-up word for when someone is proven wrong, but the point still stands.

JACK

A man who chucks work on others without doing anything himself.

JACK JOB

Lifting an aircraft with jacks.

ISOMAT

A small folding or rolling mat that you sleep on while in the field.

JACK SHACK

Jack-off station. Often a porta-shitter upwards of 120+ degrees in that bitch.

IT'S NOT GAY WITH BOOT STRAPS ON

When butt humping someone of the same sex while wearing boot straps.

JACK SOCK

Jack-off sock.

JACK WAGON

Another term for dumbass.

IVAN

What NATO countries call Russians.

JACKASSERY

Shenanigans.

IYAOYAS

The motivated war cry of aviation ordnance. "If You Ain't Ordnance, You Ain't Shit." Stolen from the YAT-YAS war cry used by AAV Marines.

JACKING

Masturbating.

JAFO

"Just Another Fucking Operator."

JAGALONE

An old way of calling someone a failure.

JAPAHOE

Japanese hoe.

JAPPER SNAPPER

Small tight Asian delicacy found outside the gates of Oki.

JARHEAD

Term for a Marine. Also one of the best war movies ever made.

JEEP

"Junior Enlisted Expendable Personnel."

JESUS PLUG

The main power cable on an AAV. Unplugging it will make the entire vehicle lose power.

JET JOCKEY

Pilot.

JERRY CAN

A five-gallon container of water or gas.

JESUS CRUISERS

Cheap flip-flops worn to keep your feet off the cum and syphilis-laden shower floor.

JEW

"Junior Enlisted Warrior."

JN

"Japanese National".

JODY

The guy who fucks your significant other while you're deployed.

JOE

"Lower Army-Enlisted."

JOE NAVY

Someone who is way too motivated to be in the Navy.

JOHNNY ROTTEN CROTCH

Dude with a dirty dick.

JOLLY GREEN GIANT

HH-3 Helo.

JOPA

"Junior Officer Protection Agency."

JUICY GIRLS

Hookers in South Korean bars.

JUMP DADDY

Jump Master.

JUMPERS, HIT IT!

Command given to Airborne personnel to execute their first point of performance.

JUNGLE ROT

Where one's feet start to fall apart due to being wet and in the jungle for so long.

JUNIOR NCO

Someone who has recently become an NCO or an NCO who is too BOOT to really understand the role of an NCO.

J-VILLE

Slang for Jacksonville, N.C.

KETCHUP AND MUSTARD STAIN

The National Defense Medal/ Ribbon that is awarded to everyone for enlisting in a time of war. The lone red and yellow ribbon resembles a ketchup and mustard stain on the uniform.

KFC

"Kentucky Fat Chick."

KICK ROCKS

Get out of here.

KICKSTAND

Someone with a huge dick. Like fucking enormous.

KILL

A response used by Marines to show acknowledgement or understanding of something.

KILL BODIES

Another response used by Marines to show acknowledgement or understanding of something.

KILL FOOT

The lead foot to kick or stomp the enemy with.

KILL HAT

The more junior drill instructors whose primary purpose in life is to make the rest of the drill instructors seem mild and laid back. They will teach drill and other things here and there but primarily they are there to fuck you up.

KILROY WAS HERE

The grandfather of tags, which started in WWII.

KINETIC

Getting violent.

KING NEPTUNE

God of the Sea and the one who grants a sailor the honor of being called a shellback.

KISS OF THE DRAGON

The steam that rises from pissing in sub-zero temperatures and kisses your cheeks.

KLICK

Measurement of 1 km or .62 miles. Feels really cool to say.

KMAGYOYO

"Kiss My Ass, Guys, You're On Your Own."

KNEE DEEP NAVY

See Puddle Pirate.

KNEE KNOCKER

Bottom part of a hatch frame or support frame of a ship that people constantly hit their shins on.

KNEE PADS

Pads used to get promoted, since sometimes promotions require you to be on your knees, generally under a desk of sorts.

KNIFE HAND

The straightened hand that resembles the blade of a knife that is often used during ass chewings. When the knife hand comes out, you know you're fucked.

KNUCKLE DRAGGER

Someone who is really dumb, like a knuckle-dragging ape. Typically, this name is reserved for infantrymen.

KNUCKLEDICK

Person with a dick as long as a knuckle.

K-POT

Kevlar® helmet.

LADY BOY

Woman who is really a man. Most of the time a prostitute. Very often in Thailand.

LALO

"Low Altitude Low Opening."

LANCE COCONUT

Slang for lance corporal.

LANCE COLONEL

Slang for lance corporal.

LANCE COMMANDANT

Slang for lance corporal.

LANCE CONDOM

Slang for lance corporal.

LANCE COOLIE

Slang for lance corporal.

LANCE CORPORAL SCHMUCKATELLI

The made-up lance corporal character used as an example by higher-ups to illustrate people fucking up.

LANCE CORPORAL SHUFFLE

A jog that's not quite a jog but looks like a jog.

LANCE CORPORAL UNDERGROUND

A secret and exclusive inteligence operation involved in passing word about anything going on in the unit, including general gossip. Be wary, if you break the code of the lance corporal underground and snitch classified information, you will be thrown out and shunned, even if you retain the rank of lance corporal. There is no getting back in.

LANCE CRIMINAL

Lance corporal. Used because of the shady things lance corporals will do.

LATRINE

Army term for bathroom.

LAND MINE

Feces from any living creature that is just waiting for you to step on it.

LAND NAV WAIVER

One who doesn't pass the land navigation course but gets pushed through training anyway.

LATRINE QUEEN

Air Force term for those in basic who are in charge of cleaning the shitters.

LAWN DART

Nickname for an F-18.

LAYO

A term for your left foot during a running cadence.

LBFM

"Little Brown Fuck Machines."

LEATHERNECK

Marines' nickname for wearing a leather collar in the 1700s and 1800s.

LEFT AND RIGHT LATERAL LIMITS

The left and right limits for your designated field of fire.

LEFT-HANDED HAMMER

Fake tool that doesn't exist in order to make a BOOT go away and look for it. Usually used because they're slowing down progress or just being annoying as fuck.

LEFT-HANDED WRENCH

Same as a left-handed hammer.

LEG

Non-Airborne soldier.

LGOP

"Little Group Of Paratroopers."

LIBO

Shortened version of liberty, more often used in casual conversation.

LIBO BUDDY

A buddy you stick with on liberty to make sure neither of you gets in trouble, lost or killed.

LIBERTY

The closest experience to freedom when you're in the military. You can take off your slave suit, leave the base, and hope you don't get caught when you are 100% violating the UCMJ within five minutes of being released.

LIBERTY BRIEF

The same few points being made over and over every week on Friday before getting released for libo. It starts with the CO telling you to stay safe, call someone if you find yourself in trouble and to not drink and drive, even though gunny's DUI got swept under the rug last week. This is followed by first sergeant and other random staff NCOs "piggybacking" off what he or she said, which really just means repeating the same things you were just told.

LICKEN CHICKEN

See Lima Charlie.

LICKIES AND CHEWIES

Pogey Bait.

LIFE OUT/LIFTED

When you're getting absolutely destroyed and chewed out.

LIFER

Someone who is doing their 20+ years to retirement.

LIGHT COLONEL

Lieutenant colonel (O-5).

LIGHT DUTY COMMANDO/WARRIOR

Someone who spends a ridiculous amount of time on light duty.

LIGHT GREEN / DARK GREEN

No matter the color of your skin, all Marines are green. Some Marines are just a darker green than others. Rest assured that all are treated just as shittily regardless of the shade of green.

LIGMA

"Lick my."

LIMA CHARLIE

Radio slang for "loud and clear." Commonly used to tell the previous caller their broadcasts are easily understood.

LIMP DICK

A broken, injured or just plain lazy person.

LISTEN UP FUCKERS, I'M ONLY GONNA SAY THIS ONCE

A term said by every platoon sergeant to convey an important message, but they will always say it more than once.

LITFU

"Lock It The Fuck Up."

LIVING THE DREAM

The term you use when you absolutely fucking hate your life and feel like painting the barracks room walls with your brains if staff sergeant fucks with you one more time, but that's too graphic, so you just use this line instead.

LN

Local national from the general population of whatever shithole country you're operating in.

LO RIGHTY LAY-O

Marine Corps marching cadence that sounds really weird at first but grows on you.

LOAD TOAD

Airmen who load ordnance. A load master.

LOCAL CLEARING BARREL

Local hoe.

LOCAL SLAM PIG

See Local Clearing Barrel.

LOCK IT UP

A more military way to tell
people to shut up. Often
used by staff NCOs to get
brownie points when someone
chuckles during the battalion
commander's speech because he
sounds like Mickey Mouse.

LONG PIG

When a human is eaten during
an extremely desperate
situation.

LOST IN THE SAUCE

When someone is totally
fucking clueless about what's
going on with no hope of
getting on track.

LOT LIZARD

Truck-stop hoe. A
motivational fuel source for
veteran truck drivers.

LOUNGE LIZARD

A female who will hang out
in the lounges or rec rooms
of a barracks waiting for
some poor soul to fill her
mouth with their dirty dick,
possibly for money or because
of their really intense daddy
issues.

LRA

"Lowest Ranking Airman."

LOW REG

A haircut that rides the
line of being in regulation.
It still goes to the skin for
about half an inch but then
quickly fades into a normal
haircut, but still checks the
box for having a haircut.
Utilized to show a complete
lack of any motivation and
in hopes to blend in as a
civilian.

LT

Lieutenant. Essentially a
private with a college degree
and the complete inability to
conduct land navigation. They
have too much power for how
inept they are, but the smart
ones will sit back and listen
to their staff NCOs to learn
how to lead.

M.A.R.I.N.E.

"My Ass Rides In Navy Equipment." Acronym designed by Navy people who are jealous of Marines.

MACH JESUS

When you're in the back of an AAV on land going 30 mph and it feels like you're going "Mach Jesus."

MA DEUCE

The M2 .50 caliber machine gun that has been a favorite machine gun across all services for decades. There's just nothing quite like slinging .50 caliber rounds at the cyclic rate and tearing shit up.

MA'AM

Greeting for a female officer or civilian.

MACHINE DUMBER

A dumb machine gunner. Which is basically all of them.

MAIL BUOY WATCH

A pretend watch out at sea to keep a shithead busy.

MAIL CALL

When they hand out your mail and it's the best feeling in the world.

MAIN SIDE

The main area of a base where most buildings and activities are. In other words, not the ranges.

MAKE A HOLE

What you say to a cluster of people to make a gap so someone or something can pass through.

MAKE IT DISAPPEAR

Get rid of something by any means possible.

MAKE THE WALLS SWEAT

When a group does PT to the point where the walls are wet.

MALINGERER

Someone who fakes or milks an injury to stay on light duty for a long period of time.

MAMA-SAN

Old woman at a bar who is a former hooker and is now in charge of the hookers.

MAN JAMMIES

The robes Middle Eastern men wear that look like pajamas.

MAN LOVE THURSDAY

Every Thursday, you and your boys are free to get as gay as you want without uttering "no homo" beforehand under the protection of "Man Love Thursday." Let it be known that if you go to bed snuggling your buddy on Man Love Thursday and wake up still spooning on Friday, that is no longer protected and you're automatically gayer than cum on a mustache.

MAN PLEASER

One who loves the taste of dick.

MANCHESTER

It's like telling your buddy "no balls" if you and your buddy were both Army Rangers. If your buddy tells you "Manchester" and you don't do it, he slaps the fuck out of you. If you accomplish the task you get to slap the fuck out of your buddy.

MANDO FUN

Mandatory fun time that is set up by the chain of command in an attempt to boost morale, but it just gets in the way of other work or your free time. It's rarely ever fun.

MANDATORY FUN DAY

See Mando Fun.

MANUALLY ADJUST

Kicking equipment to get it to work.

MARINE CORPS

The greatest fighting force the world has ever seen. They can fuck you up by land, air and sea, and have really cool dress uniforms. The Marine Corps likes to keep their Marines miserable and pissed off so they carry that rage into battle, and that's the secret sauce to their badassary.

MASTER GUNS

USMC master gunnery sergeant, or Navy gunners mate chief. One of the sickest sounding ranks if we're all being honest.

MASTURBATION STATION

See Jack Shack.

MATTIS

General James Mattis. Nicknamed: Warrior Monk, Chaos, SECDEF, Mad Dog.

MEAL ON WHEELS

Military kitchen trailer used to bring food to troops in the field. It could be worse, but at least it's usually hot.

MEAT GAZER

A piss test observer to make sure you aren't faking clean piss on a piss test, but often times they're just trying to look at your dick because they like it.

MEAT HOOKS

Hands.

MEAT SHIELD

Using human flesh as a shield from bullets or other dangerous shit.

MEAT WAGON

Field ambulance.

MECHANIZED INFANTRY

Infantry members who are attached to an armored company/battalion.

MEDIUM RARE CHICKEN

The terribly cooked food by the military.

MEERKAT OPS

When it's cold in the field so you go stand in the rays of sunlight for warmth like a meerkat.

MERITORIOUS PROMOTION

Getting promoted before meeting the requirements that are set in place for the next rank because you are shit hot.

METRIC FUCKTON

When you have more than a lot of something.

METRIC SHITTON

See Metric Fuckton.

MEU BABY

Someone who's only deployments were on a Marine expeditionary unit where you just cruise around, train, and party in foreign countries while rarely seeing any combat.

MIC GULF

Phonetic for master gunner.

MIC MIC

Millimeter.

MICKEY MOUSE BOOTS

Cold weather boots.

MID RATS

Midnight meal. Usually easily cooked food, like nuggets, fries, hot dogs, burgers, waffles or rice. Basically leftover food.

MIKE

Time-saving way to say "minute" because it's one syllable instead of two and the military is efficient like that.

MILITARY GRADE

A term used by civilians to make their shit sound strong and well-made. Anyone in the military knows their own shit comes from the lowest bidder and is usually pure shit so civilians can find much better alternatives.

MILITARY LEFT

When you are given any command that involves going to the left and you go right instead because you can't follow simple instructions, so they tell you to go to your "military left" as a way to say "correct yourself, retard."

MONKEY BUTT

Swamp ass.

MONKEY CUM

Lube for the MK-19 automatic grenade launcher.

MONKEY FUCKERS

An exercise where you bend over and grab your ankles and then repeatedly lower and raise your ass.

MONKEY SHIT

Duct seal that is waterproof and pliable.

MOOK

Schmuck.

MOON BEAM

Military term for a flashlight, because "flashlight" is too reasonable.

MOONS OUT, GOONS OUT

Phrase from the SOF community meaning they operate and own the night.

MOOSECOCK

One who has a huge dong.

MOP TOP

One who needs a haircut.

MORALE

Something that rarely exists but higher-ups must contain before it gets too high.

MOS 99Z

MOS of a combat ninja.

MOSQUITO WINGS

What the E2 rank looks like in the Army and Marines.

MOTARD

Someone who is relentlessly motivated, regardless of shitty conditions, and will go the extra mile, like wearing green on green around the barracks instead of civilian clothing, getting high-and-tight haircuts, and being way too motivated in general.

MOTIVATOR

Motivated servicemember. Word usually used by SNCOs.

MOTOR TUH

Nickname for Motor T. Transportation for personnel and equipment via trucks.

MOUTH BREATHER

Worthless POS. See Shit Bird.

MRE

"Meal Ready to Eat." Comes in a bag and consists of everything you need to have a decent meal in the field. People bitch about them, but they're really not that bad.

MRE BOMB

Where one uses an empty water bottle, puts in an unused magnesium heater from an MRE, then fills it 3/4 full of water, shakes and throws.

MRE RAT FUCKING

When someone picks through and opens up MREs to get the extras they want.

MRE SHITS

Where one shits a brick after eating only MREs for days.

MRE STOCK MARKET

Where certain MREs are worth more than others.

MUD PUPPIES

Another Coast Guardsman nickname.

MUSHROOM STAMP

When you slap someone or something with your hard cock with such force that it leaves a mark that resembles a mushroom print.

MUSTANG

A commissioned officer who was previously enlisted. Usually the smarter ones of the officers.

MUSTER

Where sailors are formed up and accounted for.

MYSTERY E

Fucked up MRE.

NAP

Non-Airborne Personnel.

NAP ROULETTE

Where one is on watch and is tired so they take a small nap in a hidden place and hope to not get caught.

NASTY GIRL

Nickname for National Guard.

NASTY LEG

Anyone who is not Airborne-qualified, especially infantry.

NAV-A-HOE

Navy hoe.

NAVY

The branch of the military responsible for transporting Marines around the globe. Stereotypically, the Navy are the gay pansies of the military, but in reality the Navy is one of the most integral and important parts of our military. Seamen will never not be gay though.

NAVY SLAVE

Undesignated sailor. A sailor with no rate who just does bitch work for the needs of the Navy.

ND

"Negligent Discharge." To fire your weapon accidentally or when it is not authorized.

NEW DICK

What females call a good looking new dude.

NIA

"Navy-Issued Ass."

NIGHT CRAWLER

Guy who shits himself six hours in-country because we weren't allowed to refer to him as "Shit Pants."

NIGHT OPS

Stealing shit from other platoons.

NINJA PUNCH

Another name for getting a non-judicial punishment.

NLT

"No Later Than."

NO BALLS

Double dog daring.

NO FUCKS GIVEN

When someone stops caring.

NO HOMO

What is said after something gay is done to attempt to cancel out the gayness.

NO IMPACT, NO IDEA

What you say when you can't see where a shot or indirect fire hit. Never want to hear that on qual day at the rifle range.

NO SCREAMING EAGLE SHIT

When the new guy PCSs from the 101st and it's all he compares shit to.

NO-SHOW JOE

When a BOOT doesn't show up to work, formation, etc.

NO TALENT ASS CLOWN

Shitty service member.

NODS

Night optical devices, or night vision goggles. Gives you a mini heart attack when you pat your cargo pocket and they aren't in there anymore.

NOF

"Non-Operating Fuck."

NON-SKID DILDO

A sailor who gets fucked over by their higher-ups and has to fill a slot of the working party, stand a watch that someone didn't show up for, or stand around hours after working while waiting for chief to say go home, etc.

NO-NECK MUFFUCKERS

People so fat or top-heavy that their neck and upper body are one.

NONER

Non-essential personnel, such as finance, commsor logistics. If they ain't on the flight line or holding a weapon, they ain't shit.

NON-HACKER

One who drops from a program.

NOT TO BEAT OFF A DEAD HORSE

Otherwise known as, "not to beat a dead horse." Something that is repeated over and over and over and over.

NOTIONAL

Hypothetical situation or entities used for training. Notionally shooting your weapon would mean aiming and saying "bang bang" instead of actually firing.

NOVEMBER GULF

"No-Go."

NOW, LISTEN UP

A precursor for a one-way conversation or ass chewing from a higher up.

NUB

"Non-Useful Body."

NUG

"New Useless Guy."

NUGGET

A young PFC who is newly in the air wing with no qualifications.

NUKE

One in the Navy who works on nuke reactors. Most of the time a book-smart but NOT street-smart sailor.

NUKING IT

A sailor who overthinks something.

NVG

"Night Vision Goggles/Gear."

OCEAN SPRAY

"The Devil's Piss." Oleoresin capsicum spray used as a non-lethal deterrent.

ODA GROUPIE

Green Beret fanboy/girl.

OFF FUCKING OFF

Not where one is supposed to be and not doing what they're supposed to be doing.

OFFICE BITCH

Lowest ranked person
in the admin office.

OFFICER CAKES

Scented urinal cakes.

OFP

"Own Fucking Program."
The best program to be on.

OH, GOOD

When you hear this from
a higher-up, especially a
drill instructor, you're
fucked, and things are
definitely not good.

OHO

"Ordinance Handling Officer."

OKI GOGGLES

When you spend too long away
from real girls so wooks or
nasty civilians seem hotter
than they actually are.
An Okinawa 9 is a stateside
4 or 5.

OKITRAZ

Another name for Okinawa,
because despite the fact
that there is no shortage of
bars, girls and things to do
off-base, Marines will bitch
about literally anything.
Part of the reason for this
is the stricter liberty
policies for people in
Okinawa, especially temporary
personnel there on UDP.

OLD CORPS

When Marines talk about how
the Marine Corps used to be
in the old days. Usually
used to describe how hard
things were when they used to
qualify with iron sights.

ON THE DOUBLE

As quickly as possible.

ON YOUR FACE

What drill instructors or
NCOs yell when they want
you to get to the push-up
position.

ONE WAY

A person who only thinks
of themselves.

OODA LOOP

"Observe, Orientate, Decide,
Act." Acronym used to teach
how to take in information
about the situation you are
faced with and make a quick
and effective decision. It
is constantly cycling because
you begin the loop over again
after each action.

OORAH

Marine battle cry to show
motivation. Often used
sarcastically because you
aren't actually motivated.

OPEN CONTRACT

Where one enters the military
without a designated job, so
they'll be put where Uncle
Sam needs them.

OPEN DOOR POLICY

When a higher-up says you can ask them something anytime. Their door is "open."

OPERATE

Basically, just doing military shit. When infantrymen and special forces are on a mission, they are operating.

OPERATION GOLDEN FLOW

Getting called from the orderly room, first sergeant, or commander's support staff to show up and sign a form followed by the joy of visiting the health and wellness center to provide a urine sample for the cause.

OPERATOR

Someone who operates or has operated. Basically, anyone who has actually used their training in real-life situations, almost always in combat situations.

OPFOR

"Opposing Forces." Many times these are people from your own unit posing as bad guys to make training more realistic. They talk shit when they kill you. Being OPFOR for training is a pretty chill job because you don't have to wear gear and get to shout "Allahu Akbar" during the training.

OPSEC

"Operational Security." Not disclosing or revealing sensitive information about operations, including administrative movements and deployment schedules that could be used by terrorists or enemy forces to target the units/personnel executing the operations. More often, used by chain of command as an excuse to get you in trouble when you mention on Facebook that you're being deployed even though the whole world already knows.

OSCAR MIKE

Acronym using the phonetic alphabet to signify "on the move." Used on the net or comms to let everyone know that you are moving.

OUTFUCKINGSTANDING

When something is better than just outstanding. Often used sarcastically when the thing you're talking about is the opposite of outstanding and probably totally fucked.

OUTSTANDING

Score for inspection or 290+ on a PFT.

OVERHEAD

The ceiling, next deck above, or in the air above.

OXYGEN THIEF

Someone who is so dumb that the oxygen that goes to keeping them alive is a waste and they're basically stealing it from the rest of us.

P-38 CAN OPENER

Old can opener for opening K-rations.

PACK BITCH

Useless. Carries everyone's shit to make up for it.

PAD EYE REMOVER

A fictional item you send BOOTs for to get rid of aircraft deckpad eyes.

PADRE

Chaplain.

PAPER PUSHERS

Admin. Rate/MOS.

PAPERCLIP

"People Against People Ever Re-Enlisting. Civilian Life Is Preferred."

PATROL SOCK

Submariner's jack-off sock.

PAUSE BUTTON

An O3-ranked lieutenant or captain, because their rank looks like a pause button.

PCOD

"Pussy Cutoff Date."

PCS

Moving from one duty station to another.

PEACETIME

When there are no combat deployments and leadership runs out of relevant things to care about so stuff starts getting really stupid. Uniform inspections take precedence over job proficiency, and infantry/combat support units lose all purpose other than going on nonstop MEU cycles.

PEANUT BUTTER SHOT

The shot of penicillin you get in your ass at boot camp. It's so thick that you can feel it get pushed in through the syringe and feels like it has the consistency of peanut butter.

PECKER CHECKER

The observers for piss tests who are required to watch the fluid leave your body so they actually look at your dick as you piss into the cup. Sometimes they will get so bored after looking at dicks for hours that they will start to mess with people and rub their shoulders or try to make them laugh as they're pissing.

PECKER INSPECTOR

See Pecker Checker.

PECKING FOR CORN

When you're trying to stay awake but can't, so your head bobs up and down like a chicken pecking for corn.

PEE PEE SMACK

Getting your ass handed to you.

PEE PIPE

Cutest way to refer to a penis.

PEN FUCK

See Pencil Whip.

PENCIL WHIP

When you don't actually do the work or inspections for a piece of paperwork but fill it out anyways. Maybe because you're too lazy or don't have the time/means to actually complete the work.

PENCIL WHIPPED QUALS

Where one gets "qualified" by someone just signing them off without proving they can do the task or know the info.

PENIS

"Personally Enhanced Nicotine Inhalation System."

PENIS PEELER

Hand.

PENIS PUFFER

Someone who sucks dick.

PEOPLE TANK

Inner hull of a submarine.

PERCUSSION MAINTENANCE

When something is broken and you don't know what is needed to fix it, you don't have the parts required, or you don't give a fuck so you just start hitting shit with a hammer or other tools.

PEW PEW

Fake gun noises that aren't taken seriously.

PFC

"Private First Class (E-2)."
"Perfect For Cleaning."
"Pointless Fucking Chevron."

PFC UP

When someone is needed for a task that probably sucks and no one wants to do it, you call for "PFC up" and one of the PFCs better fucking move to get started on it or all of the PFCs are getting fucked up.

PFM

"Pure Fucking Magic."

PHANTOM SHITTER

One who shits in weird places and is never caught.

PICKLE SMOOCHER

A brown-noser, or someone who kisses the higher-ups' wieners to get ahead.

PICKLE SUIT

Green flight suit that looks like a pickle.

PIE HOLE

Mouth.

PIECE OF FUCK

Same as piece of shit.

PIECE OF SHIT

Shitty person.

PIG

"Professionally Instructed Gunman." Member of the scout sniper platoon who has not graduated sniper school.

PIG EGG

A sandbag, tightly taped up with duct tape, used for PT. Marines will run while carrying it on their shoulders, sometimes until their shoulders are bruised.

PIGGY BACK

A term frequently used by leadership to, quite literally, repeat what the person said who just spoke before them.

PILL PUSHER

Medic/Corpsman.

PIN CUSHION

Someone whose veins are hard to find so when they go to medical for bloodwork, they have to get stuck multiple times. Coincidentally, they are usually the ones who are squeamish about needles and end up passing out.

PINEAPPLE

Old school hand grenade.

PINGER

Anti-submarine aircrewman.

PINK MIST

When you hit an enemy fighter with a bullet or explosive and they're vaporized into a pink mist of blood and guts.

PINNING

When you get promoted and they don't put the backings on your rank at the ceremony. If you're not a bitch, you leave them off for the next 24 hours so the people who are at or above that rank will punch your rank and send the sharp points into your skin.

PINNING THE HEADBOARD

The act of pressing your Airborne wings into the back of the headboard of a girl's bed after hooking up with them. This is in case the "single girl" you went home with is married or has a boyfriend who is deployed. If they are married or have a boyfriend who is deployed, that servicemember, upon returning home, will check behind the headboard to see if she was banging Jody while they were gone. This will also tell the servicemember how many dudes she hooked up with.

PIPE-HITTERS

Tier-level units who do direct action raids.

PISS COVER

Garrison cover.

PISS CUTTERS

Piss covers. Misinterpretation and poor enunciation.

PISS MATES

Two dudes who pee in the same toilet.

PISS POOR

Someone who is a poor performer.

PIT LOVE

When you make a poor shot at the qualification range, but the guys in the pits scoring your shots, mark them as hits so you get more points to go towards promotion. In most cases with POG ass-bitches, it's irrelevant because they will only shoot at the range. But for infantrymen, pit-love can be bad because poor shooters think they're good and then miss their shots when it actually counts in combat.

PITCHING A TENT

Where one's jacking off under their blanket.

PIZZA BOX

The marksmanship badge you rate when you can't shoot for shit. You will be mocked in uniform and at every ceremony. You have an RCO, stop being weak.

PLANK OWNER

Someone who is helping stand up a new unit.

PLATINUM FALCON

King of the Blue Falcons.

PLATOON DADDY

The fucker in charge of the other fuckers.

PLAY GAMES

See Fuck Fuck Games.

PLAYING FUCK FUCK

See Fuck Fuck Games.

PLEBE

Freshman at the Naval Academy.

PMCS

"Preventive Maintenance Checks and Services."

PNN

"Private's News Network."

POB

"Pat On the Back."

POCKET ROCKET

Ballistic missile warfare insignia.

POG

"Personnel Other Than Grunt." Anyone who isn't infantry.

POGEY BAIT

Snacks that people bring to the field to make field ops a little bit more bearable.

POINTY HEADS

An individual who works in a specific technical task job. Basically, anything computer.

POLE SMOKER

Someone who sucks dick or is a brown-noser.

POLE TO HOLE

Getting a stripper from her club to the bed.

POLICE

Fix something that's wrong.

POLICE CALL

Pick up brass or trash. One of the worst things to hear a higher-up suggest.

POLLY WOG

One who has not crossed the equator on a ship.

PONTI

"Person Of No Tactical Importance."

POO POND

Pond to which shit water flows.

POOLEE

Someone in the Marines delayed entry program who waits to ship off to Boot camp.

POOP DICK

A shit-covered dick.

POP SMOKE

Leave.

POPTART

An Airman whose tech school is less than 6 weeks.

PORK CHOP

Slang term for the 200-round drum of the M249 machine gun.

PORK CHOP PLATOON

Platoon of Marines in boot camp who are overweight and need extra exercise and monitoring of their diets.

PORT HOLES

Small, man-sized (barely), holes on a ship's hatch or buckle head.

PORTA SHITTER

Porta-potty. Great place to jack off, even if it's 140 degrees in that bitch. It's all part of the experience.

PORTA SHITTER ART

A genre of art specific to the military. From extensively-detailed genitalia to full walls covered in cities being destroyed by "Cockzilla," these works of art truly show that, while military members may seem like mindless robots, creativity and expression are still active in their brains.

POUND SAND

Push-ups.

POWER BOTTOM

Someone who excels or even thrives at getting fucked, both literally and figuratively.

PRC-E6

When a BOOT is sent to an E6 and told to ask them about getting radios called the "Prick E6" radios.

PRC-E7

When a BOOT is sent to an E7 and told to ask them about getting radios called the "Prick E7" radios.

PRENUPTIAL AGREEMENT

What a BOOT (or anyone) should get before they get married so when the wife fucks Jody she can't take half his stuff.

PRETTY RICKY

Well-groomed soldier.

PRIVATE

E1. Lowest Army and Marine rank.

PROFILE PATHFINDER

One who repeatedly gets injured, fakes an injury, or purposely injures themselves in order to get out of physical duties.

PROFILE RANGER

One who's at medical for various reasons all the time.

PROFILE RIDER

See Profile Ranger.

PROMOTION PADS

Knee pads used for sucking dick to get promoted.

PROP WASH

Wind coming from a helicopter's rotor blades.

PROPER GREETING OF THE DAY

What you're supposed to say to higher-ups when you pass by them. Includes "Good [time of day], [their rank]." If you don't notice them or can't tell what their black rank chevron is as it blends in with the black in their cammies, you get an ass chewing that usually begins with, "Oh, fuck me, right?"

PROPER PRIOR PLANNING PREVENTS PISS POOR PERFORMANCE

The Seven Ps.

PT

Physical Training.

PT BELT

A reflective belt, which, according to the Air Force, stops bullets.

PT RAT

One who constantly PTs.

PT STUD

Someone who is a superstar at PT. Sometimes it's through hard work, but oftentimes, it's just genetics.

PU-55-Y FORM

Form issued to someone being a pussy.

PUCKER FACTOR

A near-death experience where your b-hole puckers up.

PUDDLE HOPPER

Small prop plane like the C-12.

PUDDLE PIRATE

Term for Coast Guardsman, because they never go into deep water, only puddles.

PUKING CHICKEN

101st soldier.

PULL THE TRIGGER

Going forward with something without giving it much thought. Just going for it.

PUMP & DUMP

Smashing someone and then ghosting them immediately after. Also: "beat and yeet," "smash and dash," "cum and go," "clap cheeks and hit the streets," "dick her down and get out of town," "hit her raw," "yee haw," and "tap 'n' gap."

PUNCH OUT

One who ejects from an aircraft.

PURPLE CHURCH

A legendary strip club located just off the main gate at Camp Pendleton. Known for its frequent drunk Marines who go to see other Marines' wives dancing.

PURPLE HELMET

Head of the penis.

PUSH

Push-ups.

PUSH EARTH

Command to do push-ups.

PVT SNUFFY

Nickname for a shitbag private.

PX RANGER

A person who spends most of his check at the PX.

PX SOLDIER

See PX Ranger.

PX/BX BATTLE CRUISER

Navy version of PX Ranger.

QUEEF BUBBLE

A bubble that exits the female genitalia, whether during sex or with lots of practice through Kegel exercises. Also helps if the area is well lubricated. Often seen as part of the banana show during libo ports in Southeast Asia.

QUICK, FAST, AND IN A HURRY

When you need something done yesterday.

QUICKLIER

A dumb word even dumber SNCOs say cause they don't know how to say things need to be done quicker.

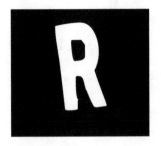

RACK

Your bed. Could be a bed in the barracks, a folding cot, an ISO mat out in the field, or the small cubbies you cram into on ship.

RACK OPS

When you're sleeping during work hours or while standing by. Some view it as a form of training requiring a unique skill set.

RAH

See Oorah.

RAIN ROOM

Boot camp communal showers.

RAKING ROCKS

Busywork junior guys are given because staff sergeant doesn't want them to fuck shit up or let them go home.

RANGE WALK

The slow walking pace while on a range due to safety.

RANGER PANTIES

Silkies. Short shorts for PT.

RANGER WIPE

When you use one piece of toilet paper to clean yourself after taking a shit by poking a hole in the paper and sticking your finger through it, cleaning your brown eye with your finger, and then wiping your finger off with your piece of TP.

RANGERETTE

One who's slept with a "Battboy."

RAT FUCK

When you take bits and pieces of something instead of taking the whole thing.

REAL ESTATE

Any physical area, whether it's on the battlefield, training in the field, or the area of the motor pool where your platoon's vehicles are located.

REAPPROPRIATE

Reusing something for a different purpose than intended.

REAR WITH THE GEAR

The people who don't go out to the field/on operations because their job requires them to stay back. Infantrymen make fun of them while bitching about how they wish they weren't in the field themselves.

RECON RANGER

Someone who believes they are, or tries to be, super high speed despite being a super POG or BOOT. They will spend ridiculous amounts of money on unnecessary gear, take moto pictures constantly, and try to convince everyone, especially themselves, that even though they're a supply clerk, they're ready to drop bodies.

RECRUIT CANDY

Name for cough drops in boot camp. Often used to cure sugar cravings and to barter.

RECRUIT LAMINATE

Using layers of packing tape to laminate important pieces of paper at boot camp as all of the recruits' belongings are constantly subjected to being thrown around and trashed.

RECRUIT TAPE

White medical tape used in boot camp for a myriad of purposes. Most often for marking things.

RECTAL ROCKET

Ass dildo.

RED CELL

Nickname for the enemy forces during a training exercise.

RED EAGLE

Archnemesis of Blue Falcon.

RED PATCHER

Landing support specialist Marines. See AIDS Marines.

RED ROCK

Funny term for Navy aviation ordnancemen.

RED TEAM

The enemy team during training exercises.

RED WINGS

Going down on a chick while she's on her period.

REDUNDANT

Most SNCOs who should've retired years ago.

REE REE

Term for someone who is a total fucking retard.

REINDEER GAMES

Good old-fashioned fuck fuck games.

REITERATE

To say something again and possibly again. Sometimes several more times.

REMF

Rear Echelon Motherfucker.

REMINGTON RAIDER

Nickname for admin Marines.

REPEAT

Asking one to say again, but can also mean to repeat a fire mission. Can get messy if used over the radio.

REPS

"Retard Positioning System."

RGR

Pointless abbreviation for "roger" that saves two letters.

RHIP

"Rank Has Its Privileges."

RICKITICK

To do something very fast.

RICKY BOXING

Jerking off in Navy boot camp.

RICKY SOCK

A duster that is actually an old sock.

RIDE THE LIGHTNING

When one gets pronged with a taser shot and "rides" the five-second lightning.

RICKY RECON

A term used to describe someone who thinks they are super high speed or tactical when, in fact, they aren't in the slightest.

RIVER CITY

Where all non-essential comms are put on lockdown during some sort of emergency for OPSEC reasons.

ROACH COACH

Food truck that shows up around base to boost morale with snacks. The food isn't that great but they have eneregy drinks, which is all you need.

ROCK EATER

A nickname for machine gunners (0331s) because they are stereotypically super dumb and super buff.

ROCK OR SOMETHING

Instructions on the MRE boxes that tell you to use "a rock or something" to lean your MRE on as it heats. Can be anything from Dwayne Johnson to anything else.

ROCK PAPER RANK

Where a senior person pulls rank during a game of Rock, Paper, Scissors to make a lower rank think there is a chance they may win and get out of work.

ROCKS AND SHOALS

Slang for Navy rules and regulations.

ROCKSTAR

Someone who is shit hot.

ROGER

Acknowledging something.

ROGER THAT

Acknowledging something but with a hint of sarcasm.

ROGUE

Someone who stays out of the limelight and is basically a ghost.

ROOF INSTRUCTOR

One who teaches corrective actions on the roof of a building so higher-ups can't hear the screams of the unfortunate souls being corrected.

ROOF RAT

Line shack rat on the flight deck.

ROOM INSPECTIONS

When rooms are inspected for either cleanliness, after field day, or they're searching for contraband and go through everyone's shit whether you like it or not. There's no guaranteed way to pass a room inspection.

ROSIE O'DONNELS

Wire cutters (dykes).

RUBBER NECKIN'

Where one's looking around and not still while in formation.

RUCK UP

When someone is told to get a little more motivation.

RUCK

The pack you carry with you on a hike. Can also be used to describe the action of hiking with a ruck on.

SACK NASTY

See Bag Nasty.

SACK OF DICKS

See Bag of Dicks.

SAFETY BRIEF

A weekly ritual where the command tells you not to do things that everyone with common sense knows not to do. You will inevitably do these when you have consumed enough alcohol to supply a bar.

SALT

A term to describe how much cool shit you've done in the service, especially in combat.

SALT DOG

One who's been around for a while and deploys a lot.

SALTY

When you've been on deployment/out in the field for a long time and your gear accumulates a residue of dried up dirt and sweat that shows that you're experienced and this isn't your first rodeo.

SALTY BOOT

A BOOT who has a non-combat deployment or MEU under his belt.

SALTY LANCE

A lance corporal who's been on multiple deployments and kicks ass but is still just a lance corporal.

SAND BAGGING

One who is purposely doing something very slowly.

SAND BOX

The Middle East.

SAND COOKIES

When you PT in the sand after getting covered in ocean water or sweat, so the sand sticks and you look like a cookie.

SAND QUEEN

Female on deployment who becomes way hotter than she usually is back home.

SANDY VAG

When a female is mad.

SARNT

Army way of saying "sergeant" within the ranks of E-5 to E-7.

SAUSAGE GRABBERS

Hands.

SAVED ROUND

Something that was supposed to be brought up but was skipped over or forgotten.

SAY AGAIN

The proper way to request a repeat of the last transmission over comms.

SCHMAMMERED

Shitfaced hammered drunk.

SCHOOL CIRCLE

When everyone forms a group huddle so someone can pass word or give instruction.

SCHWACK

To kill. Preferably with extreme violence.

SCRAMBLED EGGS

Embellishment on an officer's cap.

SCREAMING EAGLE

101st Airborne soldier. A high and tight that is higher and tighter than the highest tight. Sported by first sergeants and above. It rides the line between motivated military haircut and a mohawk.

SCREWING THE POOCH

When you have fucked something up so immensely that it is comparable to fucking a dog.

SCRIBE

Whoever has the best handwriting in the platoon and writes everything down for the platoon sergeants, commanders or drill instructors.

SCUTTLEBUTT

Gossip or a water fountain.

SEA BAG WITH LIPS

Where a chick is shaped like a sea bag, but with lips.

SEA COW

Female sailor who is a little overweight.

SEA DADDY

Senior sailor who's mentoring a junior sailor.

SEA LAWYER

A sailor who's been in a few years and thinks they know the ins and outs of the UCMJ.

SEA WOOK

Marine female on a ship.

SEAMAN TIMMY

The metaphysical sailor who is completely clueless, has no idea what's up or down, or is incredibly prone to safety hazards. Used as an example for any disaster that happens in the Navy, and has the attention span of a lima bean.

SEAT SNIFFER

Ejection seat mechanics. (AME/13B shop)

SECRET SQUIRREL

The military version of stuff that has to be kept on the down-low.

SECRET SQUIRREL SHIT

Clandestine missions to S-shops, dermo and bays to recon items for acquisition.

SECURE THAT HAPPINESS

When you're having any amount of fun and it's too much for higher-ups to handle so they tell you to go back to being miserable.

SECURE THAT SHIT

Similar to lock it up. Stop smiling, joking or any sort of communication.

SEMPER GUMBY

Always flexible. In the Marine Corps the plan can always change, the situation is never set in stone, and you always need to be prepared for the unexpected, so stay flexible.

SEND IT

Firing a round down range.

SENIOR LANCE

A lance corporal who hasn't been promoted because of closed scores, NJPs, or was an NCO and got knocked down. While they may have been in for a long time, they are still a lower enlisted Marine. They are more respected than the rest of the lower enlisted but still aren't NCOs.

SENIOR SPECIALIST

The most senior Army E4.

SEPTAR

"Seabourne Powered Target." Basically a remote-controlled sea target used for training.

SHAM ARTIST

An artist proficient in looking like they're doing a lot of work without actually doing much. They make sure they're always at the right place at the right time. They can sense an NCO's gaze, and upon that sense, they immediately produce body language that looks like they're doing stuff.

SHAM OUT

To vanish to avoid work.

SHAM SHIELD

The rank insignia that looks like a shield and identifies you as a shammer.

SHAMMER

Someone who gets out of work for fake reasons. It's an art form. The best shammers only put in just enough work to make it look like they're putting in a full workday, but really don't do shit.

SHARP

The Army's "Sexual Harassment Assault Response Prevention" resources. Intended to prevent sexual assault and harassment before it occurs.

SHAVETAIL

The haircut second lieutenants get when they're in OCS.

SHAVING BEARDS

The same as "scalping" a German, but with Hajis.

SHAVING PROFILE

Paperwork that says someone doesn't have to clean shave daily.

SHELLBACK

Someone who has crossed the equator underway and completed the shellback ceremony.

SHIP CURRENCY

Stuff or services on a ship that can be bartered for other goods or services.

SHIP WIFE

The wife you have only while out at sea.

SHIPMATE

A way to address other sailors while on ship, usually not for something good.

SHIPWRECK

Shitty sailor.

SHIT ASS

To describe a random piece of equipment or tool on a submarine.

SHITBAG

Someone who is fucked up, doesn't give a shit, and has no hope of improving. Their uniform is always a mess or barely within standards. They will skate/sham their way out of anything they can. And even if they still have multiple years left on their contract, they count down every day until they get out.

SHIT BIRD

Total disaster of a human being who sucks at everything.

SHIT FOR BRAINS

A dummy.

SHIT-HOUSE POET

Someone who writes poetry on the shitter stall walls.

SHIT ON A SHINGLE

Slang for toast and gravy but often said when something isn't going their way.

SHIT PAPER

Toilet paper.

SHIT SANDWICH

A bad situation that you're stuck with.

SHIT SHOOTER

A person who is bad at shooting.

SHIT SHOW

A situation that's totally fucked.

SHIT, SHOWER, SHAVE

The three essential steps men need to accomplish before going out, especially for a date. Never make the mistake of showering before your shit.

SHIT TICKETS

Toilet paper.

SHITTON

A lot, a really big number, or an exaggerated unit of measurement.

SHIT YOU NOT

A way to let someone know that you aren't making shit up, no matter how ridiculous it may sound.

SHIT'LL BUFF

When something isn't perfect, possibly slightly fucked, but it will be alright in the end.

SHITBALLS

A shitty situation like balls being covered in shit.

SHITCAN

To get rid of something like trash. Or someone being fired from a position.

SHITCAN LINER

Trash bag.

SHITHOUSE LAWYER

The dude you talk to from the other shitter stall who gives you advice on navigating the UCMJ to stay out of trouble.

SHITMATE

A shitty fellow sailor.

SHIT'S ALL DICKED

When everything is fucked beyond repair.

SHITSTAIN

Someone who is less than worthless and makes life harder for all.

SHITTER SKIPPER

A bad seaman.

SCHMUCKATELLI

See Lance Corporal Schmuckatelli.

SHOOTING THE SHIT

Talking with someone, usually to waste time.

SHORT-TIMER

Someone who stays in for only one enlistment.

SHOWER BABIES

When someone jerks off in the shower and some of the cum sticks around and doesn't go down the drain.

SHOWER DRAIN BABIES

Cum that is in a shower. The reason you wear shower shoes.

SHOWER JELLIES

See Shower Drain Babies.

SHOWER JELLY

See Shower Drain Babies.

SHOWER SHOES

Flip-flops or sandals worn in the communal showers to avoid any number of nasty things you might pick up.

SHUT UP AND COLOR

Another way of telling someone to do what they're told.

SICK BAY

Hospital or medical clinic. Usually where you find people trying to get out of work.

SICK CALL

Time of morning when anyone without an appointment can wait to be seen by a doc.

SICK CALL COMMANDO

Someone who goes to sick call every day trying to get out of shit. Usually there's nothing wrong with them, but maybe the doc can find something.

SICK CALL RANGER

See as Sick Call Commando.

SICKBAY BANDIT

See Sick Call Commando.

SIERRA MIKE

"Single Mother."

SIGNING BONUS

Recruiting tool to get people to enlist in hard or undermanned MOS/rates. Often times it's a trap.

SILENT SERVICE

Submarine service.

SILKIES

Now banned as official PT gear, yet still the favorite and most iconic piece of PT gear. They're very short and smooth PT shorts. You should always go at least one size too small.

SILVER BULLET

The thermometer that corpsmen shove up your ass to get your core temperature when you pass out or become a heat casualty.

SIMPLE GREEN

Clean-all solution.

SIMUNITION

Paint rounds for training.

SINCE JESUS WAS A CORPORAL

When something is old.

SITFU

"Suck It The Fuck Up."

SIZZLE DICK

Someone with herpes.

SKATE

Seek cover. Keep cover. Avoid responsibilities. Take no action. Evade. This is an art form mastered by many, especially E3s and terminal lances, where one masterfully avoids work and goes on their own fucking program.

SKATERSMATE

Same as USMC's "Skate," but Navy. Someone who avoids work.

SKELETOR

Someone who's extremely skinny.

SKIPPER

Commanding officer of a ship, squadron or unit.

SKIPPY'S LIST

List of things you're not allowed to do.

SKIVVIES

Underwear.

SKULL DRAG

An extremely low, low crawl.

SKULL FUCK

Forcibly shove your dick down their throat while grabbing their head and going to town. Most often used as a figure of speech to imply how bad you want to destroy and degrade someone. In the most extreme cases, fucking someone through their eye socket also applies.

SKY BLOSSOM

Deployed parachute.

SLACKJAW & SHITBIRD

A dumb-and-dumber scenario with two servicemembers.

SLAM PIECE

Person you're smashing, possibly on the regular.

SLAM PIG

A substandard girl who isn't your first, second, or even fifth choice. Nonetheless, it's late, and it beats jerking off for the 13th time this week.

SLAM PIG SUNDAY

After a failed weekend of not banging or picking up a chick, one resorts to a "Slam Pig" on Sunday.

SLAP DICK

One who doesn't know what they're doing.

SLAPPED ASS

Feeling or looking like shit.

SLAVE

A BOOT who gets voluntold for everything, or anyone in the Marine Corps.

SLAVE CABLE

Large black cables used to jump-start military vehicles.

SLAVE START

Jump-starting a vehicle with slave cables.

SLAVE SUIT

Military uniform because you cannot quit until the end of your contract and you are treated like a slave.

SLAW BUNNY

Nasty female.

SLAY BODIES

Infantry phrase for killing people.

SLAY FEST

A workout or a group getting disciplined so intensely that everyone is absolutely wore the fuck out by the end.

SLAY GUTS

When you're fucking a girl so hard that you rearrange her internal organs with your dick.

SLAY PUSSY

Someone who fucks a lot.

SLICK SLEEVE

A servicemember who has never deployed to a combat zone during a time of war.

SLICKY BOY

Korea slang for a thief.

SLIT TRENCH

Trench that's dug for bathroom use.

SLOOT

Slightly more polite term for a slut.

SLOW IS SMOOTH, SMOOTH IS FAST

When you rush a task, you're bound to make mistakes that will slow down the task. It can be much faster to do a task in a slower, more methodical manner. The lack of mistakes will allow you to complete the task faster than if you were to rush it.

SLUT BUCKET

A new E3 (or below) female who men expect to fuck.

SLUTBAG WHORE

See Nav-A-Hoe.

SMACKBOOK

Facebook.

SMART GUY

Sarcastic insult for someone who's not really smart.

SMASHED ASS

Where something or someone doesn't feel well or is in bad shape.

SMASHED BAG OF DICKS

See Smashed Ass.

SMEAC

"Situation, Mission, Execution, Administration/ Logistics, Command/Signal." It's a five-paragraph order for planning a mission.

SMEGMA

Liquid in the folds under a man's foreskin.

SMELL GOOD

Something that smells good, such as cologne.

SMELLING WHAT I'M STEPPING IN

When you understand what someone is talking about.

SMERT

Smart, but not smart.

SMIT

"Senior Marine In Training."

SMOKE CHECK

When you absolutely destroy someone at something by performing at a higher level.

SMOKE 'EM IF YOU GOT 'EM

A phrase said before a more relaxed brief or when the brief is gonna contain such shitty information that the speaker is trying to relax everyone before delivering shit news.

SMOKE PIT

The designated place to go smoke, frequently not adhered to. The place where much of the word passes through the lance corporal underground and E4 mafia.

SMOKE SESSION

A very intense corrective PT session.

SMOKE YOURSELF

Where one is ordered to PT themselves for correctional reasons. Can also mean to kill yourself. Sometimes they both go hand-in-hand.

SMOKING AND JOKING

Wasting time bullshitting with someone. Not necessarily while smoking, but this often takes place in the smoke pit.

SMOKING BATSHIT

When someone is so separated from reality or the realm of plausibility that the only explanation for how fucked up their train of thought is that they must be rolled up a big fat doob full of batshit and smoked it.

SMOKING LAMP

When it's clear to smoke on a ship.

SNAFU

"Situation Normal, All Fucked Up." When a situation is fucked up, but that's the norm.

SNAIL TRAIL

When a stripper or other promiscuous female is dancing/grinding on you and her wet pussy leaves a trail all over your clothing.

SNAKE EATER

Member of special forces (Green Beret).

SNAKE IN THE GRASS

A mole.

SNIPED

When one gets killed by a sniper.

SNIPER PT

Where you take your squad and go hide so you don't have to PT.

SNIVEL GEAR

Cold-weather gear.

SNOWFLAKE

Someone who gets their feelings hurt way too fucking easily.

SOAP CHIPS

Letters and notes left on dead bodies in enemy countries to demoralize combatants.

SOAPIE

A bath using a female's body to clean someone. Very popular in Thailand and the Philippines during libo ports.

SOCK BUN

The hairstyle women in the Marines are taught to wear using a rolled up sock to meet grooming standards.

SOL

"Shit Out of Luck." When the situation isn't favorable and there's nothing that can be done about it so you just have to deal with it.

SOLDIER PROOF

See Grunt Proof.

SOP

"Standard Operating Procedure." Whether or not they are followed is up in the air, but it's the way things are supposed to be done.

SOS

"Stuck on Stupid."

SOUND-POWERED PHONE BATTERIES

Another fake item used to fuck with people.

SOUP SANDWICH

When you're so fucked up that
you can only be described as
something as messy and ass-
backwards as someone trying
to put soup in-between two
pieces of bread.

SPACE CADET

Totally blanked out. The guy
you have to babysit. Even
after remedial training,
they still don't understand
their shit. They also somehow
managed to stay in.

SPACE FORCE

The newest addition to the
United States military. From
what began as a meme that
everyone joked about, to
actually becoming a bonafide
branch of our military, it is
still in its infancy stage
so we will wait to see what
happens with it.

SPACE GUN

Big fucking green crayon.

SPADES

The most popular card game to
kill time whether you are in
the field, underway, or just
standing by to stand by. The
game is iconic for Marine
mortarmen.

SPAGHETTI BLOWJOB

Giving a blowjob to
a limp dick.

SPANCTUARY

Place to jack off.

SPANK TANK

The tank in a platoon that's
designated as the only
vehicle for jacking off.

SPEARHEAD

Taking the lead in something.

SPEAR OF DESTINY

See Silver Bullet.

SQUAD BAY

A housing/barracks
arrangement where the living
area is one large open bay
with bunk beds and wall/foot
lockers.

SQUAD LEADER

The dude responsible for the
squad. He's like your dad
who's there to teach you what
to do, but at the same time
will beat the fuck out of you
when he's had too many beers
or you've fucked up.

SQUARED AWAY

When someone has their shit
together.

SQUID

A sailor by other services.

SQUIRTER

When a house is hit by a bomb and the occupants run out, still alive and sometimes on fire.

ST1

A rock.

STAB

"Selected To Achieve Business."

STACK BODIES

To kill the enemy in such high numbers that the bodies start stacking up.

STAND BY

"Wait here" until I figure out what the fuck is going on, or "You fucked up big time and you better prepare to have your soul crushed."

STAND BY TO STAND BY

Fancy way to tell someone they need to wait because they're about to get fucked.

STAND FAST

Don't move yet but be prepared to. A drill command that will distinguish which squads are to remain stationary while the other squad moves.

STAND THERE AND LOOK PRETTY

When you're working with someone and you don't have anything for them to do so they just have to stand there and watch you work.

STAPLE GUNNER

Admin clerks. The only rounds they send down range are staples in roster paperwork.

STARS

"Soldiers Totally Against Ranger School."

STAY FROSTY

Stay alert.

STEAL

"Strategic Transfer of Equipment to Alternate Location."

STEEL PUSSY

Steel wool.

STOCKADE

Military prison or brig.

STOLEN VALOR

Someone who poses as former military or pretends to have earned awards they didn't earn.

STORE THAT IN YOUR GRAY MATTER

Remember that shit, and make sure you know it because it will be important in the future.

STRATEGERY

President Bush's version of "strategy."

STUMP

"Stupid Tankers Under Mortar Protection."

STUPID FUCK

A fuck who is stupid.

SUCK DICK FOR BEER MONEY

When one is down on their luck and the only way to get some extra cash before payday would be to suck dick.

SUCK HOLE

A mouth.

SUCK IT THE FUCK UP

To keep moving forward when times are hard.

SUCK IT UP, BUTTERCUP

See Suck It The Fuck Up.

SUCK START

Put the barrel of a gun in your mouth and blow your brains out.

SUCKING ON CASPER

Falling asleep with your mouth open.

SUGAR COOKIE

Where one is to roll in the sand or dirt during PT-ing, then continue PT only to look like a sugar cookie themselves. There's also a sandhill named after this term in Twentynine Palms.

SUPER BOOT

Not just any regular BOOT, but a BOOT who has embraced his position to the fullest and will live up to every terrible stereotype of a BOOT.

SUPER HOOCH

A chick who is a superwhore.

SUPER MOTO

One who is far too motivated and actually drains motivation out of everyone else.

SURF 'N' TURF DINNER

A special meal, usually on Fridays, especially on the ship, to boost morale. Steak and lobster/crab legs are the go to items.

SUSIE ROTTENCROTCH

A character used to describe the nasty girls who live around military bases and get run through like Tiananmen Square.

SWAG

"Scientific Wild Ass Guess."

SWAMP ASS

A sweaty ass.

SWEEPERS

Designated time on a ship to clean. Also XO's happy hour.

SWINGING CLIT

Referring to the amount of females present and available to help with something.

SWINGING DICK

Referring to the amount of people present and available by the count of their dicks, although it's not necessarily only referring to the males.

SWINGING WITH THE WING

The assumption that working in the air wing is skate as fuck, and they party 24/7.

SWORD FIGHTERS

Where two guys piss in a toilet and "fight" with their pee streams.

SYNC PARTY

When all the radios are synced at once.

T.A.R.F.U.N

"Things Are Really Fucked Up Now."

TAB CHASER

A female who only fucks guys with tabs (SF, Ranger, Airborne, Sapper, etc.)

TACTICAL GAGGLE

Something that went tactically wrong.

TACTICALLY ACQUIRE

It isn't stealing. It's taking ownership of something that doesn't belong to you, without getting caught, of course.

TACTICOOL

Carrying extra, useless gear in the hopes of looking high speed.

TAG CHASER

Girls who specifically go after military guys in hopes of marrying them for the benefits.

TAILBOARD JOCKEY

One who rides the back part of a fire truck.

TALK OFFLINE

To speak privately about a personal issue, usually when you mess up.

TAMPON

A reservist who only comes in once a week, every month. Like a tampon.

TANGO UNIFORM

See Tits Up.

TANKER BAR

A big-ass bar used to pry open shit.

TANKER STEW

A massive shit a tank crewman lets out after being stuck inside the vehicle all day.

TAP RACK BANG

Sequence for clearing a weapon malfunction. Tap the magazine to make sure it's in all the way. Rack it back to make sure the chamber is clear and a new round is inserted. Then pull the trigger to make sure the weapon fires.

TARP BOOTY

When it's raining in the field and you rail out a female underneath a tarp.

TENT BOOTY

Fucking a female in the field.

TERMINAL LANCE

When your MOS cutting score is so high or constantly closed and it is nearly impossible to get promoted, so you just accept that you will be a lance corporal until the day you get out, and then probably get mailed corporal six months after you're out.

TERMINAL SELECT

When you get selected for corporal in the months following your EAS.

THAILAND

A country with pretty much no rules. You can blow up a cow with an RPG, watch a girl shoot darts out of her pussy, and drive Go Karts down the freeway while chugging beers.

THANK YOUR RECRUITER

When your career isn't going the way you planned and it's "not your fault."

THE FUCKENING

When things are going too good and one's lower-enlisted senses activate, warning them of immediate fuckery that's going to be dropped on them from higher up at any moment.

THE ISLAND

Marine Corps Recruit Depot Parris Island.

THE MAFIA

Group of people from the Philippines who joined the Navy.

THE WIZARD

Psychologist.

THROAT PUNCH

The desire to strike someone in the area of the neck between the chin and chest. Usually associated with someone using fewer brain cells than they were born with.

THS

"Tiny Heart Syndrome."

THUD FUCK

Hitting someone directly with a 40mm grenade close enough that it doesn't detonate.

THUNDERCUNT

Super bitch.

TIGHT

A sarcastic response commonly used by Drill Instructors to say something is definitely not good.

TIGHTEN UP THAT SHOT GROUP

Where one's shot group is all over the place and needs to be tightened up.

TIME NOW

When you need something done right fucking now.

TIMEPIECE

A watch, of course.

TITS ON A FISH

Useless.

TITS UP

When something fails or dies.

TLAR

"That Looks About Right."

TNT

"Tactical Nap Time."

TO ALL WHO SHALL SEE THESE PRESENTS, GREETING

The opening statement to an award citation usually read by an SNCO with a speech immpediment. You're gonna be standing at attention for a good while.

TOES TO THE LINE

Where one lines up with their toes to the line.

TOMFUCKSTICK

A name used for pretty much anyone you work with who you already know somewhere, somehow, at some point in time, will certainly fuck something up and get you yelled at for it because they are a useless piece of shit.

TONGUE PUNCH

Where one uses their tongue to go down on a chick from the front or back.

TONY HAWK

Someone who's a professional at skating out of work.

TOO EASY

A precursor to either something bad or good that's about to happen.

TOOL BAG

Douchebag.

TOP

Top ranking dude in charge of shit.

TOPSIDER

The one who dishes out the fuckings.

TORE UP FROM THE FLOOR UP

Someone who is drunk.

TOTAR MUH

It's like Motor T except more retarded.

TRACKIN'

To understand.

TREE LINE

Could be a literal tree line, but more often any place that is out of sight for a NCO to take you to either smoke you or beat your ass without getting caught.

TRENCH MONKEY

Someone in the Army.

TRICARATOPS

Another form of dependa.

TRUNK MONKEY

Rear gunner on a vehicle convoy.

TUBE PUNCH

Getting checked for an STI.

TUBE STEAK

Dick.

TUBE STROKER

One who jerks off SNCOs or officers for their own gain.

TUNDRA WOOKIE

Female Marine out in the cold.

TURBO

Someone who gets things done really fast.

TURD BURGLAR

Someone so low and despicable they will steal your turds.

TURDALICIOUS

Good motherfucking food!

TURDBUILDER

Food.

TURDNUGGET

Shitty worker or person.

TURN TWO

Turn to two o'clock and carry out the plan of the day.

TURTLE FUCK

When you smack someone in Kevlar® with Kevlar®.

TWIDGET

Sailor who repairs electronic equipment.

TYFMS

"Thank You For My service.

TYFYS

"Thank You For Your Service." Usually used in text form in a sarcastic way when someone unnecessarily mentions their service, as if they're just hoping to be thanked.

UMOP

"Ugliest Motherfucker
On Post."

UN-ALIVE

To murder someone and take
their aliveness away.

UNASS

To unfuck. Repair.

UNCLE SAM'S CANOE CLUB

A term for coasties via
Navy sailors.

UNDER THE RADAR

Out of sight, out of mind.

UNDERWATER BASKET WEAVER

A sailor or Marine who has
completed dive school.
Therefore, rates to wear
"dive bubbles."

UNDERWAY GOGGLES

When you're underway at sea
and females are way more
attractive all of a sudden.

UN-FUCK YOURSELF

To get your shit together.

UNIFORM GROUPIE

A person who follows people
who wear a certain uniform.

UNSAT

Not up to standard.

UPPER DECKER

When one shits in the
toilet's water reservoir.

VAPE PEN

Pen filled with nicotine or other substance.

VERBALLY ASSIST

Screaming at someone until they get the mission accomplished.

VET TV

Veteran Entertainment Television. Imagine if Comedy Central deployed to Afghanistan. That's us. We're the blatantly offensive military streaming service that brings the darkest and most irreverent military stories to the big screen. Stream on all your favorite devices and start laughing to get to get over the bad times. Because laughing is better than killing yourself. Right? And when you sign up for an annual subscription, you get a limited edition t-shirt for free. Go to VeteranTv.com to learn more.

VETFLAKE

Someone who gets out and constantly complains about civilians on social media. Was probably a shitbag when they were in, but they don't do anything with their life when they get out so their entire life revolves around their military experience.

VOICE IN THE SKY

On-base, loudspeakers used for emergencies.

VOLUNTOLD

Being forced to do something, but they make it sound like you're volunteering.

WACK SHACK

See Jack Shack.

WAFFLE ASS

One with a flat ass.

WAFFLE STOMP

To push shit through a shower drain with your foot.

WAFFLE TOP

Grid-fleece thermal top that's issued as gear. Popular cold weather gear. The grid pattern and tan color make it look like a waffle.

WAG

"Wild Ass Guess."

WAG BAG

Toilet kit to shit in. Consists of a plastic bag with kitty-litter lookin' shit at the bottom and a zipper-lock bag to pack it up after you've used it for easy disposal.

WAGNER LOVES COCK

Common graffiti found throughout Marine Corps bases because Wagner does love cock.

WAITLIFTING

Working out while waiting for word.

WALL-TO-WALL COUNSELING

See 4 Wall Counseling.

WAR MACHINE

Refers to any up-armored vehicle made to absolutely fuck the enemy.

WAR PIG

A woman who loses all sense of femininity once she joins.

WAR TROPHY

Body parts taken from slain enemy fighters such as ears, fingers or teeth.

WAR TURTLES

The tortoises found in Twentynine Palms. They've seen some shit.

WARHEADS ON FOREHEADS

A plane's ordnance dropped on the enemies' foreheads.

WARM AND FUZZY

Being confident in your understanding of orders or the mission.

WASTE OF AIR

One who is useless.

WATER AND IBUPROFEN

The cure to any and all ailments in the military. Back pain? Crushed hand? Leg blown off? You guessed it. Water and ibuprofen should have you fixed.

WATER BUFFALO

The large storage unit for potable drinking water that is brought to the field to resupply water.

WATER BULL

See Water Buffalo.

WATER DOG

Water filtration specialist. Known for being jacked because they have so much free time to get swole in the gym since they don't really do anything.

WATERWALKER

Waterdogs. Marines whose job is to purify water.

WE'LL GET OFF EARLY

You will definitely be working past whatever the estimated end time is because fuck you.

WEAPONIZED AUTISM

The weapons platoon of an infantry company.

WEAPONS DRAW

Where one gets their weapon from the armory, usually four hours before step-off.

WEED

Forbidden fruit.

WEEKEND WARRIOR

Reservist or National Guardsman because they pretty much only work on weekends.

WEENIE WATCH

Piss test observer who looks at your weenie to make sure there's no funny business.

WEST PAC WIDOW

A wife whose sailor or Marine goes out on a West Pac cruise.

WHACK SHACK

See Jack Shack.

WHALE JIZZ

See Whale Sperm.

WHALE SPERM

Lube for MK19 machine gun grenade launcher.

WHALES

Fat dependas when they go to the beach.

WHISKER FRISKER

Mustache.

WHISKEY DICK

Where one's dick doesn't work due to drinking too much whiskey.

WHISKEY LOCKER

The storage room at bootcamp where all the cleaning supplies are stored.

WHISKEY LOCKER BREW

Alcohol the "House Mouse" has stolen from the drill Instructor hand-stored in the whiskey locker for safe keeping.

WHISKEY PETER

Water-proofing.

WHISKEY PIG

The recruit in charge of organizing the storage locker at Boot camp.

WHISKEY TANGO FOXTROT

"What The Fuck."

WHITE KNIGHT

Someone who tries to do the right thing.

WHITE SPACE

When there is time between scheduled activities filled with pointless training for the sake of doing something.

WHITE TORNADO

When a white servicemember pulls his dick out and spins it around.

WIZ QUIZ

A drug test.

WHORE BATH

Wet-wipes bath.

WIG SNAP

Getting shot in the head.

WILCO

Will copy.

WILLIE PETE

M34 white phosphorus incendiary/smoke grenade.

WINDEX JUNKIE

Someone who strictly uses Windex for field day.

WINDOW LICKER

A fucking idiot.

WING IT

Doing something without a solid plan and hoping everything works out.

WITH THE SPEED OF A THOUSAND GAZELLES

Fast. Very fast.

WIWA

The person now in civilian work or Guard/Reserve complaining, "When I was active duty, this is how we did it."

WIZZO

Weapons service officer. Back-seater in a jet.

WM

Derogatory. "Woman Marine" or Walking Mattress." Interchangeable with the female Marines who sleep with most of their unit.

WOFTAM

"Waste Of Fucking Time And Money."

WOG

Pollywog who has not crossed the equator.

WOLF PUSSY

A term in the artillery community that refers to the cloud of smoke that escapes from the howitzer when a round is fired.

WOMAN

"Warrant Officer Mandatory Afternoon Nap."

WOMB BRUSH

Slang for the giant Q-Tip things used to clean howitzers. They get in there deep. Really, really deep.

WOOBIE

Also known as a poncho liner. One of the greatest pieces of military equipment that people who actually go to the field are sure to cherish. It's a blanket, sleeping bag, pillow, poncho liner, and general source of happiness, especially for grunts.

WOOK

"Women Outside Of Kitchen." Derogatory. Female Marine. They're called wooks for two reasons. Their grooming standards allow for them to have long hair, similar to wookies from Star Wars.

WOOKIE

See Wook.

WOOKIE MONSTER

See Wook.

WOOLLY PULLY

An issued, scratchy, ugly, uncomfortable sweater issued by the Marine Corps to wear over service uniforms.

WORD

Info about the plan of the day, pertinent information on things coming up in the future, or any kind of direction that is coming down the pipeline.

WORKING PARTY

A group put together to accomplish a task. Usually the task is pointless. Never volunteer for these. They aren't really a party.

WRINKLE BOMB

An older woman who fucks servicemembers.

WTI

"Worse Than Iraq."

YAM YAS

"You Ain't Mechanics, You Ain't shit!" Term used by dumbass POGs who fix things.

YAOYAS

See IYAOYAS.

YARD SALE

When a servicemember is EASing so they host a sale of their military gear and pocket pussies.

YAT YAS

"You Ain't Track, You Ain't Shit." The autistic cry heard when in the vicinity of Amphibious Assault Marines. Originated from grunts calling their amtrackers "shitheads" during the Vietnam War and the trackers affectionately adopting the title.

YEET

The act of throwing something when the only concern is distance, not accuracy.

YOO-HOO

A term retarded SNCOs use
to get your attention.

YOU CAN'T FIX STUPID

You can provide
instruction, direction, and
motivation, but sometimes
you have a turd who cannot
accomplish his assigned
task as he or she simply
lacks the mental capacity
required to complete it, no
matter how simple it may
be.

YOU DON'T RATE

When you are too BOOT to
qualify for something, like
getting a low fade haircut
or blousing your boots
extremely low.

YOUR GOOD FOOT

The left foot you first step
with when marching.

YUCCA MONSTER

Any ugly bitches in or around
Twentynine Palms or Yucca
Valley. Sometimes referred
to as Desert Yetis.

YUCK MOUTH

Complete lack of oral hygiene,
probably needs to visit the
dentist yesterday.

YUMA YETI

Same as a Yucca Monster,
but in Yuma.

YUT

"Yelling Useless Things."
Poking fun at all the
ridiculous things that are
used as a response. The go-to
response of the unmotivated.

ZARF

"Z-Axis Retaining Frame."
A cupholder on a submarine.

ZERO

A term used in Marine Corps
Boot camp when the drill
instructor wants all recruits
to freeze in place.

ZERO DARK RETARDED

A dumb hour to be tasked with
anything in the middle of the
night/early morning.

ZERO DARK STUPID

When something is stupid
early in the morning.

ZERO DARK THIRTY

A generic name for the middle
of the fucking night.

ZERO FUCKS

Not caring.

ZIP

Zero.

ZJ

A sexual favor you can't afford.

ZONE OF ACTION

Small section of a larger area.

ZONK

Actually keep that a secret.

ZOOMIES

Pilots or aircrew in the
Air Force.